PEAKLAND RIVER VALLEY WALKS

Tony Stephens

Published by Sigma Leisure – an imprint of
Sigma Press, 1 South Oak Lane, Wilmslow, Cheshire SK9 6AR, England.

British Library Cataloguing in Publication Data
A CIP record for this book is available from the British Library.

ISBN: 1-85058-450-8

Typesetting and Design by: Sigma Press, Wilmslow, Cheshire.

Cover photograph: The River Wye from Monsal Head

Maps and photographs: The author

Printed by: MFP Design & Print

Preface

As a youth who lived on the banks of a river in the Yorkshire Dales, I cannot remember a time when I was not beside, on or in a river. In London, where I went to sing as a chorister at Westminister Abbey, the river was a horrid chocolate colour, but my first serious study of maps started there, reading copies of *The Dalesman* during sermons.

For the past 15 years my family has lived within striking distance of the Peak District. In many ways the Peak District is a more compact version of the Yorkshire Dales, and I have come to regard it and its rivers with equal affection.

A couple of years ago I began to realise not only what good walks the Peak District river valleys provided but also that, since the rivers are so close together, the river valleys make an excellent way of systematically exploring the Peak District. When I approached Sigma's Graham Beech, I was delighted that he was of the view that the river valleys walks would make a worthwhile subject for a book.

Before the summer of 1995 there could hardly have been a better one than that of 1994, with weeks on end of good weather, to walk all the rivers in the Peak District. I am grateful to my wife and friends who were willing to have their arms twisted to accompany me on some of the walks. I am particularly indebted to Walter Thorpe who also appeared at both ends of the camera.

A few of the rivers walked while writing this book were new to me but, to my surprise and delight, each one of them turned out to be interesting and worthy of inclusion.

I can now only hope that my readers derive as much pleasure from the walks as I have done.

Tony Stephens

Rivers of the Peak National Park

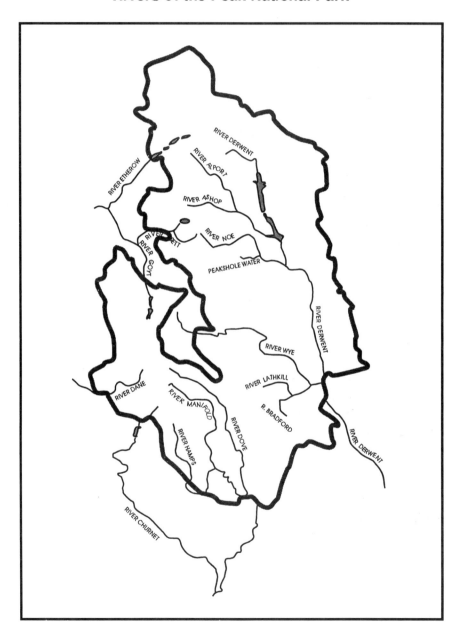

Contents

Introduction

Walking the River Valleys   1

Geology and the formation of the Peak District Landscape   6

The Walks

Walk 1: River Ashop   11
  Hayfield to Ladybower reservoir: 12.4 miles

Walk 2: River Churnet   19
  Morridge to Leek: 6.9 miles
  Leek to Froghall: 11.6 miles
  Froghall to Rochester: 9.4 miles

Walk 3: River Dane   34
  Danebower Quarry to Rushton Spencer: 10 miles

Walk 4: River Derwent   44
  Howden Reservoir to Bamford: 9.6 miles
  Bamford to Baslow: 8.4 miles
  Baslow to Rowsley: 4.6 miles
  Rowsley to Cromford: 8.6 miles
  Cromford to Whatstandwell: 2.9 miles
  Slippery Stones to Howden Edge: 10 miles
  Calver to Eyam via Offerton and Highlow Halls: 6.2 miles
  Stanage and Carl Work: 7.7 miles
  Curbar Gap and Baslow Edge: 3 miles
  Cromford Canal to Wirksworth: 4 miles

Walk 5: River Dove   **79**
   Axe Edge to Hartington: 9.6 miles
   Hartington to Thorpe Cloud: 7.7 miles
   Thorpe Cloud to Rocester: 9.7 miles

Walk 6: River Etherow   **95**
   Crowden to Hadfield: 5.6 miles
   Hadfield to Compstall: 6.6 miles
   Reservoir circular walk: 7.5 miles

Walk 7: River Goyt   **106**
   Derbyshire Bridge to Whaley Bridge: 8.4 miles
   Whaley Bridge to Compstall: 9.6 miles

Walk 8: The River Hamps   **117**
   Morridge to Weags Bridge: 12 miles

Walk 9: Rivers Lathkill and Bradford   **123**
   Lathkill and Bradford Dale circular: 10.5 miles

Walk 10: River Manifold   **134**
   Axe Edge to Hulme End: 9.8 miles
   Hulme End to Ilam: 8.8 miles

Walks 11.1 and 11.2: River Noe and Peakshole Water   **149**
   Hayfield to Brough: 12 miles
   Hope valley circular: 8 miles

Walk 12: River Wye   **163**
   Topley Pike to Monsal Viaduct: 6.4 miles
   Monsal Viaduct to Rowsley: 10.4 miles

Appendices

Social and Economic Development   **178**

Plants in the Peak District   **187**

Walking the River Valleys

No other area in Britain, as compact as the Peak District, combines so much natural beauty with a wealth of geological, historical and industrial interest. Undoubtedly the best way to explore this fascinating area is through those features which define its landscape – its river valleys.

This book describes some 250 miles of excellent walking along 15 Peak District river valleys. Because the rivers are so close to one another, nearly all of the interesting parts of the Peak District are explored. The rivers covered are shown on the map preceding the contents. While most are within the Peak National Park, three rivers have been included which lie mainly just outside its boundary on the western periphery – the Churnet, Etherow and Goyt. Each river valley has its own distinctive character, perhaps the best known features being:

¤ the "Edges" of the upper Derwent

¤ the cave systems of the Hope valley

¤ the landslips of the Ashop and Alport valleys

¤ the swallow holes of the rivers Manifold and Hamps

¤ the limestone pinnacles of Dove Dale

¤ the floral diversity of Lathkill Dale

¤ the towering limestone cliffs of the Wye.

Equally delightful, however, are the lesser-known valleys such as the Churnet, Dane and Etherow and some of the river tributaries. In each valley, the walks have been carefully planned to include both the best quality walking and visits to the many places of interest.

The valleys and hillsides of the Peak District have been important transport routes back into pre-history. In the late medieval period, an extensive system of packhorse routes was established. Because these packhorse routes were rarely suitable for later upgrading to turnpikes, the legacy is left of a superb network of footpaths and bridleways. This allows all of the main river valleys of the Peak District to be walked with very little need to set foot on a roadway. This network has been added to in the 20th century when many later transport systems, such as railways and canals, have been converted into paths and cycle tracks.

The walks are described going downstream from the river source. Where a source is up in the hills, the walk normally starts in an adjacent river valley. Although much of the walking is along the valley bottoms, for most valleys there is at least one climb to higher ground. Few hill-tops are over 500-800 feet above the valley floor. With a relatively painless climb, a different perspective is gained, not only over the valley below, but also of the wide panoramas so characteristic of the Peak District.

The walks are divided into 12 chapters. Although most of the chapters describe a single river valley, there are three exceptions:

  ¤ the Alport is too short to be described separately and is included as a part of the Derwent valley walk

  ¤ a circular walk covers both the Lathkill and the Bradford rivers

  ¤ the Noe and Peakshole Water (better-known as the Edale and Hope valleys) are brought together in a single chapter, since some of the best walks are along the watershed between the two valleys.

Each chapter comprises four sections:

(i) a brief summary of the character of the valley, and of the walk

(ii) a series of maps

(iii) a detailed description of the walk

(iv) more detailed background information on the "places of interest" in the valley. These include places both directly on, and adjacent to, the walk.

The purpose of structuring the information in this way is to reduce the amount of reading needed on the walk. This allows you to choose whether to access the additional information when on the walk or at a more convenient time (for example, in bed).

The information in "Places of Interest" is cross-referenced to the maps, the reference number being shown within a circle. Thus, you will find 1.4 circled on map 1.2 next to the Snake Inn. In "Places of Interest in the Ashop/Alport Valley" you will find the relevant entry under "1.4 Snake Road and Snake Inn."

The maps have been drawn so that the walks start at the bottom of the page and progress upwards. Whilst this may at first seem strange to the Western eye, which is used to reading from the top of the page, it has the very considerable benefit that the relative position of places on the ground and on the map in front of you are the same. No more turning maps upside down!

Wherever possible, strip maps are used, similar in style to those made for the roads by the 17th century cartographer Ogilby. These allow two maps with 10-15 miles of walking to be fitted onto a single page. The aim here is to minimise the number of times you need to move between pages. Not all rivers oblige by flowing for any distance in the same direction (the Hamps flows in every direction except west in its short journey from source to confluence). In such circumstances there is no avoiding the use of a wider map. For each river, the maps are numbered consecutively so that you will move from one map to the next as you progress down the river valley.

The symbols used should be self explanatory, with a consistent set of line thicknesses used to differentiate between river, walk, path, road, canal, woodland, reservoir etc. Perhaps the only symbol needing further explanation is the "special" direction symbol.

You will see that the direction of progress along the walks is indicated periodically by a "standard" direction symbol ($\rightarrow$). At the beginning and end of many of the maps, but not necessarily at the exact edge, you will notice a single "special" direction symbol ($\Rightarrow$). These symbols mark the same place on adjacent maps, and are particularly useful where there is an overlap of maps due to a change of orientation.

The scale of the maps at 1 inch to the mile has been chosen as the best compromise between giving a good overview and sufficient detail for navigation purposes. While the scale chosen is probably adequate for 90% of the 250 miles described, for some of the less walked and signposted areas, such as the upper reaches of some of the smaller rivers, much larger scale maps are desirable.

It would not be practical to include maps at this scale in the book and, where necessary, you should augment these maps with 2½ inch Ordnance Survey maps (1:25,000). Fortunately, two such maps cover nearly the entire area of the walks in this book: Outdoor Leisure 1, The Dark Peak and Outdoor Leisure 24, The White Peak. These maps are particularly good, showing detail down to the individual field boundaries. They enable you to see exactly which route to take to find the concealed stile at the other side of the field. This can save a lot of retracing of footsteps and also avoid inadvertent trespass.

For a few of the walks, it is possible to contemplate completing the whole river valley walk in one session (and it is very satisfying to do so). For most however, it is anticipated that sections or circular walks will be tackled. (A luxury is to walk with friend(s) so that a linear walk may be planned). The longer walks have been split into sections of no more than about 10 miles, choosing break points which have car parking nearby. Most of the valleys have more frequent parking than this. In general, car parking should not constrain you from planning the length of walk to suit your taste.

On the maps I have indicated the main car carks only. Most valleys also have many other places where a few cars may be parked. With a few exceptions, I have not marked the smaller parking places, to avoid risking a few of them becoming overused.

Because so much of the landscape may be only understood in terms of the underlying geology, there is a short introductory section on the geology of the Peak District immediately after this introduction. There are also two Appendices at the back of the book with additional information on the Economic Development and the Flora of the Peak District.

Much interesting archeological material from the Peak District is housed in two museums which are well worth a visit; Weston Park Museum, Sheffield and the Buxton Museum and Art Gallery. Perhaps if you plan a walk and the weather turns inclement, these are places to which you should divert.

Although walking in the Peak District is an all-the-year round activity, you should be aware that the more elevated areas receive little of their annual hours of sunshine during the six months between October and March. (Buxton receives less than 20%!).

It would not be possible to list the very large amount of reference material I have drawn on in researching this book but I would like to make a special mention of "Peakland Roads and Trackways" by A.E. and E.M. Dodd. This fascinating book traces the origins of roads and tracks in the Peak District back into pre-history. Roads will never look the same once you have read this book. Unfortunately, it is now out of print and therefore unless you can find a second-hand copy, you may like to consider "Walking Peakland Trackways" by Mike Cresswell (published by Sigma Leisure).

Finally, for those who enjoy the countryside but have yet to make acquaintance with the Peak District, I can only say that much that delights awaits your discovery.

The author

Geology and the formation of the Peak District landscape

Three hundred million years ago, Northern England was a shallow tropical sea located just north of the equator. Some two hundred miles to the north was a land mass of continental size. Into this sea was deposited the enormous amount of limestone material seen in the White Peak area of the Peak District and the Craven area of North Yorkshire.

The limestones of the Peak District are of two main types

¤ "bedded" limestones over most of the central plateau

¤ "reef" limestones around the margins of the "bedded" limestones.

It is thought that the "reef" limestones were formed in a similar manner to the modern barrier reefs.

Following the formation of this limestone basement, there was a period when deltaic rivers similar to today's Mississippi and Nile rivers flowed off the continental landmass depositing silts and grits varying in thickness from 500 to 5000 feet. The surface of these deposits must have been a shallow marshy area with dense primeval forest cover, for the gritstone layers are interspersed with the coal measures on the western edge of the Peak District.

The period when these limestone, gritstone and coal measures were laid down is known by geologists as the Carboniferous. By the end of the Carboniferous period most of the rocks of the Peak District had been brought into existence, although their sculpting and the formation of our rivers has been the result of two subsequent events; earth movements towards the end of the Carboniferous Period and erosion during the Ice Ages.

The earth movements were the result of major mountain building in Western and Central Europe. Although Britain was towards the edge of the area of influence, it nevertheless experienced extensive stressing. The effect of this stressing differed from area to area. To the north of the Pennines there was extensive faulting with whole areas being lifted thousands of feet relative to the neighbouring land. One of the best-known of these is the Craven fault seen exposed at Malham Cove. In the Peak District, the effect was the formation of a large dome. There was also considerable buckling of the rocks towards the west of the Peak District. This may be seen in the jagged gritstone outcrops of the Roaches close to the source of the Churnet and in the limestones exposed in the Manifold valley at Ecton.

Much like an onion which has had a slice removed from its surface, the Peak District dome has been eroded exposing limestone at the centre and areas of gritstones and coal measures at the periphery.

Rocks deposited on top of the Carboniferous rocks have left little trace in the National Park since they have been subsequently eroded. Just outside the Park however, on the western and southern periphery, softer red sandstones of the Triassic period are the dominant rock types, formed when the Peak District was an arid desert. These rocks are seen on the River Churnet walk, downstream of Leek and below Thorpe on the River Dove.

How and when the river valleys of the Peak District were sculpted as we see them today is the subject of some conjecture, but it is thought that this happened in relatively recent geological times during the Ice Ages. The landscape is consistent with the glaciers and melt waters from these glaciers being the primary agents responsible for the formation of the valleys.

There have been three periods of glaciation during the last million years. The second Ice Age had the greatest effect on the formation of the Peak District landscape, with ice extending down the Dove, Derwent and Wye valleys.

Although the last Ice Age (50,000-10,000BC) subjected the Northern Pennines to considerable erosion, the Peak District was towards the periphery of the ice sheet and escaped the erosion seen further north. It is for this reason that the dales of the Peak District are less barren that those of the Craven District of Yorkshire.

In many of the Peak District valleys there is a distinct change in the landscape as the river flows out of a broad valley into a much narrower gorge. The change is due to an increase in hardness in the underlying rocks. Thus, at Hulme End on the Manifold, Hartington on the Dove and Matlock on the Derwent, we see the valleys narrowing as the river flows into limestone. The reverse is the case at Thorpe on the Dove and below the reservoirs on the Etherow. Here the rivers enter softer rocks and the valleys widen. The agents for these changes were not the rivers themselves but rather glaciers and glacial melt waters.

A number of the river valleys where the rock type is shale have substantial landslips. Whole hillsides have been subject to slippage in the valleys of the Ashop, Alport and Noe. The largest landslips are to be seen at Alport Castles and Mam Tor. Alport Castles is now believed to be stable but Mam Tor remains active. This is to be seen in the highly distorted main road below Mam Tor which had to be abandoned in 1979.

Shales have caused considerable problems for the construction engineer during the industrialisation of the Peak District both because of the threat of landslippage and also because of the possibility of encountering noxious gases trapped in the formations. Both were real dangers for the lead miners when dewatering their mines and in more recent times have caused problems for road, railway and water engineers.

Since early Victorian times, when the connection between clean water and public health became apparent, the water engineers have shown particular interest in the valleys of the Peak District. Several valleys inside the National Park have been dammed and others have been seriously considered at various times. Unstable ground conditions caused a number of dams just to the east of the National Park to fail catastrophically in the 19th century with the loss of several hundred lives. Even the recent building of the Carsington reservoir was considerably delayed due to a slippage.

In several of the valleys, there is evidence that the river courses have been modified as a result of moraines deposited by glaciers. At New Mills on the river Goyt, a moraine across the former river bed diverted the river and forced it to cut a new channel through the hard gritstone of the Torrs. Similarly, the Derwent has only flowed through Chatsworth since the blockage of a more westerly channel through Bakewell.

It is not always appreciated that, in addition to the sedimentary limestone and gritstone rocks, there are extensive intrusions of volcanic rocks into the Peak District. For many years, volcanic material was quarried for road building at Calton Hill (Wye valley).This abandoned quarry, which is now a council tip, has some outstanding volcanic formations including hexagonal pipes, and has been designated as a site of special scientific interest (SSSI). Other examples of volcanic rocks which may be seen on the walks include River Wye (in Millers Dale and Tideswell Dale, also an SSSI), River Lathkill (below Lathkill Lodge) and River Derwent (near Bonsall).

Stone walls are an important visual feature of the Peak District and some such as those at Roystone Grange have been dated back to Roman times; subsequent farmers merely building on top of the original base. The majority of the Peak District stone walls however are the result of 17th and 18th century enclosure and much may be deduced from them of the land use at the time of enclosure. At the one extreme we have the very narrow strip fields such as those at Chelmorton, reflecting land use at what was originally an Anglo-Saxon settlement. At the other extreme are the very large fields at the bottom of the Manifold valley in the region of Throwley Hall; scenery more typical of a medieval monastic grange. Since walling material is expensive to transport, most is of very local origin and is therefore a good indicator of the underlying geology. A wall of mixed rocks is normally a good indication of a transition from one rock type to the other.

The limestone areas of the Peak District are heavily mineralised, particularly with lead, but also with copper (Manifold and Hamps). Although these deposits, which were previously of considerable economic importance, have now been worked out, minerals associated with lead such as calcite and fluorspar are still being worked today.

Tufa, a most unusual mineral of no economic importance, is still being formed in a few places. Tufa is a calcium carbonate deposit formed as a result of bacterial action in the presence of moss and algae. It may be seen at one of the dams in Lathkill Dale and there is a unique house made from the material in the Via Gellia.

Not all the waterflows in the Peak District are on the land surface. In the limestone areas there are extensive systems of underground passageways and caverns, some formed by prehistoric rivers and some still in the process of being formed by present underground waterflows. Both types of feature may be seen by the public in the caverns of the Hope valley. The rivers Manifold and Hamps are famous for disappearing underground only to reappear several miles downstream after flowing underground for about a day.

In other areas there are fissures in the limestone which are so deep that the water on its underground travels is heated by coming into contact with hot rocks. The resulting thermal springs have been used to establish warm water baths at Buxton, Matlock, Bakewell and Stoney Middleton. Perhaps not surprisingly, the most success-ful of the baths were those with the warmest waters (Buxton and Matlock). These were sufficiently successful to be important factors in the development of the towns.

Walk 1: River Ashop

Distance: 12.4 miles (13.1 miles via Alport Towers)

Ordnance Survey map: Outdoor Leisure 1, The Dark Peak

Starting point: Kinder Bank Car Park, Hayfield SK 048869

The Ashop valley has been an important transport route back into antiquity, with the Roman Road following what was probably an even earlier route. Today the route is known as Doctor's Gate. Because of the difficulty of the terrain, the modern Snake Road was one of the last turnpike roads to be built. It features regularly in weather reports on account of its vulnerability to snow.

A feature of both the Ashop and the adjacent Alport valleys is a geology which has led to extensive landslides. One of the most dramatic landslides in Britain may be seen at Alport Castles.

Perhaps the least inhabited of all the Peak District valleys, the Ashop makes a fine high walk across almost the width of the Peak District. The first half of the walk is particularly isolated and is accessible only to the walker. Because of the elevation of the walk, there are some exceptional views (particularly from the top of William Clough and from near the end of the walk). To do full justice to these, the walk should be done on a day when there is good visibility.

Because of the inaccessibility of the source of the Ashop, the walk starts at Hayfield in the adjacent Sett Valley. Only after a steep climb up William Clough is the source reached at Ashop Head. The walk then follows the Snake Pass under the Edge of Kinder Scout before joining the Roman Road at Lady Clough which descends the valley to Alport Bridge. Below Alport Bridge, there are the two alternatives of either following the main route down the valley to the Ladybower Reservoir or taking a detour to visit Alport Castles.

Parking is available at the start (Hayfield), middle (Lady Clough above the Snake Inn) and the end of the walk (Ladybower Reservoir). This gives the option of either doing the walk in two halves or completing it in one outing.

The River Ashop from the Snake Path

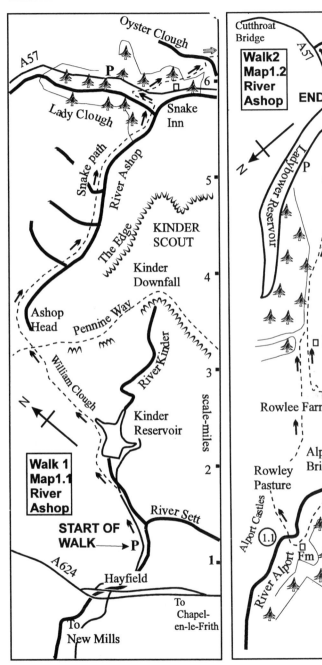
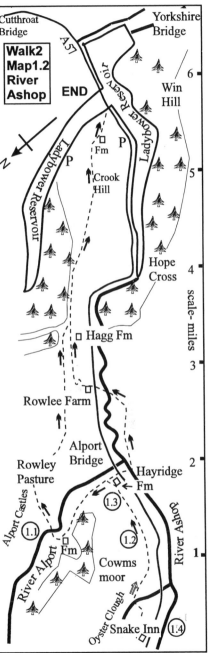

William Clough

The Walk

The car park at the beginning of the walk is in an old quarry. It was from this quarry that the famous Mass Trespass of 1932 started (see the plaque on the rock face). This is now acknowledged as the single most influential event in the establishment of the National Parks.

From the car park, take the road up to the reservoir and the path around its western edge. Some thousand feet above is the Kinder Downfall (at its best after heavy rainfall and in high winds when the falling water is atomised).

From the most northerly point of the reservoir, the path climbs William Clough, steepening considerably over the shale at the top. At this point, you have climbed some nine hundred feet since leaving the car park and, on a clear day, there are good views back down the clough to the Cheshire plain in the west and Axe Edge in the south west.

The scenery changes abruptly at the top of the clough to a flat peat landscape. The Pennine Way is crossed as it descends from Kinder Scout. The source of the Ashop is reached at Ashop Head where the path turns eastwards. Here, the Ashop is a mere brook and has a reddish colouration. In several places there are "shows" of oil coming out of the shale.

Follow the Snake Path for about another two miles. The Edge of Kinder Scout is some 600 feet above. As the path descends steeply to the woodlands at Lady Clough, you are approaching the Snake Road.

At Lady Clough, turn left to follow the tributary of the Ashop upstream. The path swings right in a clearing to take you up to the main road. Take the path into the woodlands at the other side of the road. This path emerges from the woods into the open in just under half a mile. (The Snake Inn is below you on the main road. If you wish to visit the Inn, there is a forest path which leads back to the main road which starts just before the point at which the walk leaves the wood).

Refreshed, take the path back to the top of the wood. From here to Alport Bridge you are largely following the line of the old Roman Road from Brough to Glossop. If the visibility is good, it should be possible to see almost to the end of the walk from the edge of the woodlands. Two small hillocks, some six miles away (Crook Hill), mark the point where the path starts to descend to the Ladybower Reservoir.

After the wood, there is something of a scramble down a steep slope to Oyster Clough where a stream is crossed. Careful inspection of the hillside ahead shows that its undulations are the result of landslippage.

The path crosses Cowms Moor and, just before the path meets the Snake Road at Alport Bridge, Hayridge Farm is reached. Here the old Roman Road goes through the farmyard. Follow the path to the left until a path to your right takes you down to the river at Alport Bridge. If you wish to visit Alport Castles, which is one of the most impressive landslips in Britain, follow the track up the Alport valley (as described in the Derwent walk). From the Castles a path across Rowlee Pastures rejoins the valley bottom walk at Haggside.

The valley bottom route crosses the Snake Road at Alport Bridge, before crossing the Ashop just upstream. About half a mile down the valley from this footbridge, leave the path which is climbing ahead to Hope Cross and bear left down to the river. Cross a culvert which is carrying water extracted from the Ashop to the Derwent.

Cross the Ashop at the Rowlee Bridge. From the bridge up to the main road the minor road is fenced and it is interesting to see that, in the absence of grazing, a few oak, ash and birch have established themselves. This is the natural flora of the valley and, in the absence of sheep, would cover the entire valley floor.

Cross the main road and climb past Rowlee Farm with its 1849 datestone. Above the Farm, the road zigzags tightly as it ascends another landslide to higher ground. The path from Alport Castles rejoins here, and you take the path ahead signposted to Crookhill Farm.

Ahead, there is a wood to your left for approximately a mile and the last section of the wood is rather tedious. There is no view to the left because of the wood and none to the right because of the slope of the land. However, you will be rewarded on leaving the wood by some exceptional views. The very best viewpoint is from the small knoll which is the highest point. Here, some 600 feet above the reservoirs, there is a panoramic view to which no photograph can do full justice. You should be able to see:

¤ to the head of the Derwent – Howden Edge and Outer Edge

¤ across the Derwent to Derwent Edge

¤ down the Derwent to Stanage, Hathersage and Millstone Edge

¤ back up the Ashop to the woods around the Snake Inn

¤ Kinder Scout

¤ Win Hill

¤ up the Noe to Lose Hill, Mam Tor and Rushup Edge.

It is worth considering, as you view the eastern side of the Peak District, that a few miles away at the top of William Clough, you were viewing the panorama of the western side. Within such a short distance, you have been able to see the ground where nearly all the rivers in this book rise. This illustrates one of the delights of the Peak district – its compactness.

The path ahead is to the left of Crook Hill and, when the farm is reached, signs take you to the left of the farm buildings. The path then descends to the reservoir just north of the road bridge where there are several car parks.

Places of interest in the Ashop and Alport valleys

1.1 Alport Castles

The geology of the Ashop and Alport valleys comprises gritstone resting on shale. The formation of the valleys during the Ice Ages left the hillsides in an extremely unstable condition, unable to bear the weight of the rocks above. This led to widespread landslippages throughout the two river valleys. Alport Castles, the largest of these landslips is one of the most dramatic in Britain. The Alport Tower is a large column of material which has moved into the valley. It is thought that the slippage was progressive rather that catastrophic and has now stabilized.

1.2 Doctor's Gate

After the Romans left Britain, many of their roads were used by the Saxons. The road at the bottom of the Ashop valley was a way to a market or a "portway". This usage is reflected in the name Alport. In medieval times, the road became known as Doctor's Gate after the 16th century Dr John Talbot. Dr Talbot, the vicar of Glossop, was the illegitimate son of the Earl of Shrewsbury. The road took his name because of the frequency with which he used the road when travelling between Glossop and his father's castle at Sheffield.

The danger of road travel in medieval times is suggested by the name of a bridge to the east of Ladybower Reservoir. In 1635 a traveller was found here with his throat cut and hence the name; Cutthroat Bridge.

1.3 The Roman Road

The Roman road from Glossop to Brough runs down the Ashop valley before climbing to Hope Cross. The walk generally follows the line of this Roman road between the Snake Inn and Alport Bridge. The road has been excavated at a number of places along its length and was a flagged way four feet nine inches wide. A short stretch of original paving is to be seen closer to Glossop on Coldharbour Moor (see *Peakland Roads and Trackways* by A.E. and E.M. Dodd; now out of print).

1.4 Snake Road and Snake Inn

Although it is reasonable to guess that the road takes its name from its sinuous nature, it is actually named after the Duke of Devonshire who was the main financier of the turnpike road. The family crest of the Devonshires is a snake.

The Snake Road, a turnpike road from Glossop to Sheffield, was only authorized by an Act of Parliament in 1818. One of the last turnpikes, it was built by the famous engineer, Thomas Telford. Although technically a success, it was a commercial failure. It was unable to recoup its very considerable capital cost before the railways started to take away its customers.

The Snake Inn was opened in 1821, shortly after the completion of the road, as a Coaching Inn and a tollgate. The highest turnpike road in Britain, the Snake Pass is usually one of the first roads to be affected by snow. Photographs in the Inn show just what depths of snow can be encountered.

Walk 2: River Churnet

Distances:

Total: 27.9 miles

Section 1: Morridge to Leek: 6.9 miles

Section 2: Leek to Froghall: 11.6 miles

Section 3: Froghall to Rocester: 9.4 miles

Ordnance Survey maps: Outdoor Leisure map 24, The White Peak; Landranger 118, 119 and 120

In comparison with the nearby Dove and Manifold, the Churnet is little-known outside Staffordshire. Its wealth of scenery, industrial archeology and accessibility to the walker justify much better recognition. A particular attraction is that it still remains largely inaccessible to the motor car.

The Churnet rises in the rugged gritstone area to the west of Leek. It flows for most of its length through softer red sandstone in a river valley carved by glacial melt waters from Lake Dane, a large lake which, at the end of the Ice Age, was situated to the north of the present Rudyard Reservoir.

Much of the valley has a flat alluvial bottom and, because of this, few paths have been established directly adjacent to the riverbank. However, this lack of footpaths is more than compensated for by a combination of canal towpaths and former railway tracks. These allow most of the valley to be walked in close proximity to the river.

There is some interesting industrial archeology at Froghall, where the walk follows the line of one of the earliest railway lines in the country. A detour around Oakamoor allows a visit to the very attractive Dimmingsdale.

Some parts of the Churnet can be rather muddy in wet weather, including

– between Frith Bottom and Meerbrook (map 2.1)

– the canal feeder between Leek and Wall Bridge (map 2.1)

– between Denstone and Rocester (map 2.3).

Dimmingsdale

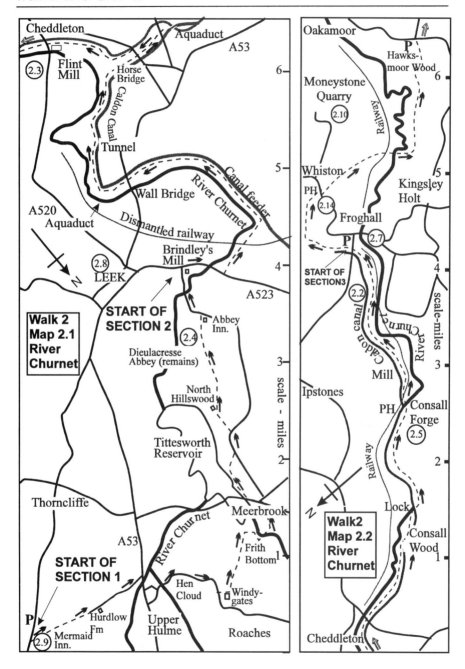

Walk 2 Map 2.1 River Churnet

Cheddleton
Aquaduct
A53
2.3 Flint Mill
Horse Bridge
Caldon Canal
Tunnel
Wall Bridge
River Churnet
Canal feeder
6
5
Whiston
PH
2.14
Froghall
P
2.7
Oakamoor
P
Hawks-moor Wood
6
Moneystone Quarry
2.10
Railway
Kingsley Holt
5
A520 Aquaduct
Dismantled railway
Brindley's Mill
2.8 LEEK
N
START OF SECTION 2
Abbey Inn.
2.4
Dieulacresse Abbey (remains)
North Hillswood
Tittesworth Reservoir
Thorncliffe
River Churnet
A53
Meerbrook
Frith Bottom
Hen Cloud
Windy-gates
START OF SECTION 1
P
Hurdlow Fm
Mermaid Inn.
2.9
Upper Hulme
Roaches
A523
scale - miles
4
3
2
1
Ipstones
START OF SECTION3
2.2
Caldon canal
River Churnet
Mill
PH
Consall Forge
2.5
Railway
Lock
Consall Wood
Walk2 Map 2.2 River Churnet
N
Cheddleton
scale-miles
4
3
2
1

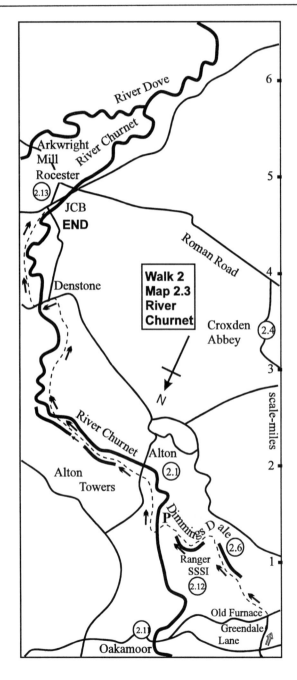

The Walk

Section 1: Morridge to Leek

Distance: 6.9 miles

Starting point: Mermaid Inn, Morridge SK037605

Map: 2.1

For the first two miles, the Churnet runs through an Army Training Ground and the river is inaccessible. The starting point for the walk is chosen as the Mermaid Inn, on an old drovers' road high above the Churnet valley. On a clear day, there are exceptional views looking down over the Ramshaw Rocks and The Roaches. Parking at the Mermaid is reserved for patrons, but there is limited roadside

Drovers' road near the start of the Churnet walk

parking opposite the Inn and additional parking a short distance down the road in the direction of Leek.

Two paths descend the undulating hillside from the Mermaid Inn to Upper Hulme. Take the more southerly path (towards Tittesworth Reservoir) which passes through Hurdlow Farm. You are now following, in reverse, a length of the 18th century drovers' road from Congleton to Nottingham.

Just before Hurdlow Farm, you will join a farm track which takes you down to the bottom of the valley. Turn right at the main road and follow the A53 for a short distance before taking the road into Upper Hulme. In Upper Hulme, follow the road past the Works towards Hen Cloud.

Below Hen Cloud, a farm road leads down to Windygates, a fine Hall of 1634. Although the road is private to traffic, it is a public footpath. Before the turnpike was built in the 18th century along the line of the present A53, the road from Leek to Buxton took this steep incline past Windygates.

The path crosses in front of Windygates and then along the top edge of the barn. Turning left, the path goes diagonally downs the field to a stile and then over open undulating fields using stiles as signposts. The Staffordshire Moorland Way is joined and, just before reaching the reservoir, the path is forced to the right to detour around a stream coming down to Tittesworth. Follow the path until a farm road is reached at Frith Bottom and then bear left over the stream. At the first gate after the stream, take the path to the left. Follow the edge of the fields to a small farm. The farm lane leads to a minor road where you turn left to Meerbrook. Here turn left again and pass the Lazy Trout Public House to reach the reservoir.

Take the path which skirts the western edge of the reservoir until a small road is reached in about half a mile. This is the road which was cut when the reservoir was flooded. Take this road and shortly the Leek to Meerbrook road is reached. Turning left towards Leek, in about a quarter of a mile, take the road left over a cattle grid. This leads to a farm called North Hillswood. Just before reaching the farm, take the track which climbs to the right bypassing the farm building. At the top of the hill, the path passes a small coppice on the left.

Tittesworth reservoir

The path now proceeds down the hill with the site of the old Cistercian Abbey of Dieulacresse on the left. Little remains of the Abbey which is on private land. Just before reaching the Abbey Inn, notice the ancient "hollow-way", a track leading back towards the Abbey. Inspection of the exposed rock shows that you have now left the Millstone Grit and entered an area of Bunter Sandstone. This is the predominant rock type of the rest of the Churnet.

At the Abbey Inn, turn left to join the road into Leek. Before the building of the turnpikes this was the main road from Leek to Macclesfield and was the road down which Bonnie Prince Charlie's army marched in 1745 during the abortive attempt to seize the crown. Follow the road as far as the bridge over the Churnet. The last cottage before the river is reached is called Mole End. Notice that in this area the river is above the level of the valley bottom and a "mole" or bank is required to channel the river towards the Mill.

Follow the river down towards the main A523 where Brindley's Mill is on the corner. James Brindley is regarded as the father of the canals, being responsible for the construction of some 400 miles of waterway which were of such importance to the industrialisation of England. A Derbyshire man by birth, he was a millwright before becoming a canal builder and had strong connections with Leek. The Mill is well worth a visit if open. Notice the name of the pub at the other side of the A523. The Dyers Arms reflects the importance of the dyeing industry to Victorian Leek.

Section 2: Leek to Froghall

Distance: 11.6 miles

Starting point: Brindley's Mill Leek, SK 978569

Maps: 2.1 and 2.2

Leave the Mill along the A523 towards Macclesfield. Pass the factories on the right-hand side and proceed up the hill. Although the road is busy, there is an adequate footpath. Less than half a mile from the Mill cross the A523 and take the signposted footpath across the fields on the left. The line of the dismantled railway is soon crossed and the path proceeds across the fields towards the hillside. You are now walking across a very flat plain which is clearly of alluvial origin and the river is running at the left. At the hillside there is a small fast flowing culverted stream. The water has come six miles from the River Dane via Rudyard reservoir and is the feeder which will flow into the Caldon canal in another two miles.

Turn left and follow this feeder. For a short distance there are three watercourses running in parallel. The next mile and a half is a most attractive walk along the edge of the wooded slope.

The A53 is reached at Wall Bridge and there are other names with Wall in their title in this vicinity – Wall Grange, Wall Hill. Wall is a word often associated with Roman roads. Although the only road in the Leek area fully authenticated as Roman is that to the east between Buxton and Leek, it is possible that this was the Roman Road out of Leek to the west, leading to a camp at Chesterton.

The canal feeder crosses under the A53 and, in another half a mile, runs into the Caldon canal. What appears to be a fine bridge over the Churnet is actually a former aqueduct (taking the canal a further half a mile into Leek). This last section has now been infilled.

In about another half mile along the canal bank, there is a short tunnel. The path climbs over the hill to rejoin the canal on the other side of the tunnel. About a mile after the tunnel, the Horse Bridge is reached. Turn left and then, after a short stretch of road, turn left again onto the canal spur which goes to Cheddleton. (If time allows, it is well worth carrying straight ahead at the Horse Bridge to Hazelhurst junction. Here there is some of the most interesting canal architecture in the country, with the Cheddleton and Leek canal spurs crossing each other before coming together).

Whichever route is chosen, now proceed along the canal towpath to Cheddleton. On the left, just before the road bridge in Cheddleton is the Flint Mill built by Brindley.

After Cheddleton, continue to follow the canal towpath. In approximately two miles, when Consall Wood is reached, the canal and river merge into a single waterway for the next mile to Consall Forge. Consall Forge has a pub, The Black Lion, and is an attractive area which is popular with walkers.

At Consall Forge the river and canal separate. Follow the canal towpath towards Froghall. On the way, you will pass another Flint Mill, now derelict. Unlike Cheddleton with its waterwheels, this Mill was later driven by a turbine.

At Froghall the towpath is the boundary of the sprawling works of BICC. This is a direct descendent of the copper industry established in the valley in the 18th century. The canal terminus at Froghall has been converted into a most attractive picnic area by the Staffordshire County Council, with much interesting archeology to explore including lime kilns, loading bay and tramways.

Section 3: Froghall to Rocester

Distance: 9.4 miles

Starting point: Froghall basin SK027478

Maps: 2.2 and 2.3

On the tourist display at the canal terminus, several local walks are suggested. Initially, take the blue route up the tramway towards the

Caldon Quarries. (Before leaving the terminus area you will pass a sign to the right to Whiston. This was a tramway which brought copper down from Whiston, where ore from the Duke of Devonshire's mines at Ecton on the Manifold was smelted (see Manifold walk 10.1)).

About a mile up the Caldon tramway, take the blue track across the fields on the right towards Whiston. The track zigzags somewhat, but eventually the road is reached at Whiston just below the pub. The pub has some interesting photographs of the Whiston Copper works and its demolition. After researches in the Lounge Bar, follow the road towards Froghall for a short distance before turning left into Ross Lane. Pass a farm (Eavesford) and, when the lane divides, take the right fork which leads down to the Churnet.

Take the bridge across the river and the path across the field. At the end of the field you should turn left to follow the Staffordshire Way down the valley. For the first three-quarters of a mile the path is in close proximity to the river but, thereafter, passes East Wall Farm and climbs through Hawksmoor Wood. When the track divides in the wood, take the branch to the right which take you to Hawksmoor Cottage on the Oakamoor to Cheadle road. At Hawksmoor Cottage take the road ahead, Greendale Lane, to Old Furnace where a track is met which leads down into Dimmingsdale.

The next two miles down Dimmingsdale is a well-known beauty spot with a succession of picturesque lakes in a broadleaf woodland setting.

At the bottom of Dimmingsdale, cross the road and take the bridge over the Churnet to join the path down the old railway line towards Alton. The station at Alton is in the Italianate style by the famous Victorian architect Pugin. Almost opposite the station the former Brass Mill is worthy of inspection.

After Alton, follow the track to Denstone. The railway was built in 1845 largely on the infilled former Froghall to Uttoxeter branch of the Caldon canal. In a number of places, however, the railway was not built directly on the line of the canal and the former canal bed is still clearly visible at the side of the path.

On reaching Denstone, turn left down the B5032, pass over the bridge and then turn right to take the path across the fields towards

Rocester. Just before reaching Rocester the path climbs from the river bank to the edge of the hill. The view in front of you is dominated by the massive JCB works set beside its lake. To the left, the church and Arkwright Mill are on the Rocester skyline. Both the path across the fields and up the side of the hill can be very muddy in wet weather.

Places of interest in the Churnet valley

2.1 Alton and Alton Towers

Alton is the 19th century seat of the Earl of Shrewsbury. Features of interest include the castle remains, the Italianate railway station by A.W.N. Pugin, the lock-up and the Brass Mill. There is reputed to be a dark side to the history of the mill with the bars manufactured here being used as a form of currency in the slave trade. Alton Towers is the second biggest tourist attraction in Britain.

2.2 Caldon Canal

In 1769 the Trent and Mersey Canal Company acquired the Caldon Low mineral rights and applied to parliament to build a tramway from Caldon to Froghall and extend their canal from Etruria to Froghall. The Act made clear that the purpose of the canal was to develop the Staffordshire Mines and the Cheshire saltfields. The Canal Company employed James Brindley as its surveyor and, although he died during the project, his brother in law completed it in 1779.

The canal was extended first to Leek in 1797 and to Uttoxeter in 1811. The latter extension was shortlived for, in 1845, the railway company, which also owned the canal, decided to build a railway down the valley to Uttoxeter. Down to Froghall, the railway ran in parallel with the canal but from Froghall to Uttoxeter it was decided to infill the canal. The new railway ran largely on the line of the old canal.

In building the 1797 extension to Leek, the canal was not merely accessing Leek but was perhaps more importantly seeking an additional water supply. This supply was drawn from a reservoir built by the canal company at Rudyard. The origin of this water was the

River Dane. The Churnet valley was, at the end of the Ice Age, formed by glacial meltwaters from Lake Dane. It is paradoxical that the endeavours of the 18th century canal builders should establish a supply of water to the Churnet from the Dane, restoring a position which existed when the river valley was first formed.

2.3 Cheddleton Mill

Brindley's Flint Mill of 1770 may be seen at Cheddleton. The Mill processed flint into slip for the pottery industry and was operational until 1963 (see Manifold walk 10.6 and Wye walk 12.2). It is now a museum.

2.4 Cistercian Abbeys: Croxden and Dieulacresse

In the 12th and 13th centuries there was a rapid expansion in the foundation of Cistercian Houses. Two abbeys were founded near the Churnet, largely because of the suitability of the area for sheep rearing; Croxden in 1179 and Dieulacresse in 1214. Both these abbeys had very large endowments of land on which they raised

Croxden Abbey

sheep and traded wool into Europe. By the late 13th century the sheep flocks numbered 7200 at Croxden and 4800 at Dieulacresse.

Practically no building fabric remains at Dieulacresse, presumably because the proximity to Leek made the recyling of the stone attractive. Croxden on the other hand has extensive remains and is open to the public.

2.5 Consall Forge

Although there is now no archeological evidence to be seen on the ground, there was an iron forge at Consall Forge in the 16th century. Iron making later became uneconomic in the Churnet valley but, with the coming of the canal in the 18th century, Consall Forge became one of the major centres for the making of lime. The derelict kilns may be seen at the canal side. Consall Forge may only be reached on foot or by canal. With its waterways, bridges and pub (The Black Lion), Consall Forge is an attractive area and is popular with walkers.

2.6 Dimmingsdale

Dimmingsdale is a picturesque valley with lakes and broadleaf woodlands. For a hundred and fifty years the valley was a centre for iron and lead smelting and is one of the earliest examples of industrial reclamation. It was returned to its rural state by the Earl of Shrewsbury who in the 18th century, lived at Alton Castle. The Earl laid out the paths to form an attractive woodland coach drive for his guests.

The valley is probably at its best in late spring for, in common with many similarly ungrazed riverbanks, by July the foliage has grown to a height which obscures the water in some places.

2.7 Froghall

An important industrial archeological site with lime kilns, tramways and canal terminus. Froghall was a lime processing site between the opening of the Caldon canal in 1793 and the closing of the Caldon tramway in 1920. BICC still operate a works at Froghall.

This is the successor of copper working at Whiston which started in 1776.

2.8 Leek

This is the major town of the Churnet with its traditional industries of textiles and dyeing. Known as the Queen of the Moorlands, Leek is today the home of the Britannia, one of the top ten Building Societies, and is a major centre for the antiques trade. Much of the architecture is Victorian and was undertaken by one family (W Sugden and his son). The church dates back to Norman and possibly Anglo-Saxon times (there is an Anglo-Saxon cross in the churchyard).

An unusual phenomenon may be seen from the church yard between June 20-22, when the sun sets twice. The first sunset is behind Bosley Cloud and shortly afterwards the sun re-emerges, only to set a second time over the Cheshire plain.

2.9 Mermaid Inn and the Drovers' Road

In the 18th century large numbers of cattle were driven long distances to the growing city markets. A drovers' road crossed the Peak district, passing through Meerbrook and then over Morridge. Cattle were driven down this road, normally in herds of 200, to Nottingham. The Mermaid Inn, then known as Blakemere House, was a drovers' inn.

2.10 Moneystone Quarry (near Oakamoor)

The material extracted from this quarry is a red sandstone. After chemical treatment, it yields a pure white sand which is used in the glass industry. Until relatively recently, the sand was conveyed down the to the river and transported out of the valley by train. Road transport is now used.

2.11 Oakamoor

Oakamoor is a pleasant village with a couple of pubs. The site of the Thomas Bolton Copper Works which processed copper from the Whiston smelters is next to the river. The first transatlantic cable was manufactured here in 1856. The Works was demolished in 1963 when operations were transferred to Froghall and the site was converted into a picnic area.

2.12 The Ranger (SSSI)

On the north side of Dimmingsdale is an ancient hill pasture at The Ranger which has been designated a Site of Special Scientific Interest. The ancient pastureland here is grazed to maximise the plant life (which includes the round leaved sundew).

2.13 Rocester (see River Dove walk, 5.8)

2.14 Whiston

Copper from the Duke of Devonshire's mines on the Manifold was worked here from 1770 to 1890. When the works were demolished, the stone was used to build the church. Pictures of the Works and its demolition may be seen in the local pub.

Walk 3: River Dane

Distance: 10 miles

Ordnance Survey map: Outdoor Leisure 24, The White Peak

Starting point: Danebower Quarry SK 008698

This delightful short sandstone valley runs roughly east to west. With its open moorland, intermittent fingers of deciduous woodland and enclosed valley bottom from which the motor car is excluded, the Dane valley is ideal for walking.

Three Shire Heads

The walk generally follows the Cheshire/Staffordshire border downstream from close to its source on Axe Edge, passing on the way:

– Three Shire Heads, a delightful packhorse bridge at which the three counties of Cheshire, Staffordshire and Derbyshire meet.

– Lud's Church, a massive cleft in the gritstone caused by a landslip

– Danebridge, a place where the pub once served Bonnie Prince Charlie's army but now slakes the thirst of walkers.

Bosley Cloud at the end of the walk is some 600 feet above the Cheshire plain and is probably the best vantage point from which to view the plain. On a clear day there are extensive views right over the plain to the Welsh Hills beyond.

There is no evidence of prehistoric man in the valley and the earliest settlements are two monastic sheep granges (Wincle and Swythamley). The valley is reputed to be the setting for the medieval epic poem "Sir Gawain and the Green knight".

In the Industrial Revolution, both the Dane (at Gradbach) and its tributary the Clough Brook (at Wildboarclough) were harnessed for textile production and between them the mills employed nearly a thousand people. With the demise of textile manufacture, no other industry was established in the upper Dane which reverted to its former rural economy.

There are car parks at Gradbach and Rushton Spencer and road-side parking at Danebower Quarry (the start of the walk), Danebridge and Bosley Cloud (the end of the walk). The last of these has only a restricted amount of parking and an alternative is to retrace your steps to the car park at Rushton Spencer. Indeed, the walk from Rushton Spencer to The Cloud and back makes an excellent short outing in its own right.

A word of warning: following heavy rain, some of the Dane valley walk can be extremely muddy. Not impassable, but only recommended to those who don't mind mud on top of their boots! The worst sections are:

– between Gradbach and Danebridge (map 3.1)

– the canal feeder (map 3.1)

– Raven's Clough (map 3.2).

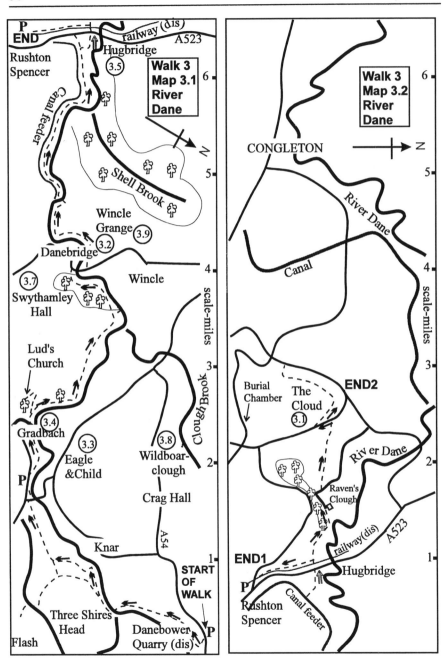

The Walk

The walk starts at the derelict Danebower Quarry adjacent to the A54, where there is some roadside parking. By the side of the path going down to the river is a stone chimney which was associated with a coal mine. On first sight, there appears to be no flue to take the hot gases into the chimney. Closer inspection shows that the hearth is further down the hill, near the river. The hot gases ran in a channel underground. Where there has been a collapse, it is possible to see into this channel.

From the quarry, follow the river downstream for about three quarters of a mile to the packhorse bridge at Three Shire Heads. In periods of wet weather, one area on this path can be boggy requiring "tussock hopping".

As its name suggests, Three Shire Heads is the meeting point of three counties – Cheshire, Staffordshire and Derbyshire. Several packhorse routes converged on this bridge and, if you look underneath, you will see that the original bridge has been widened. With its attractive pools and packhorse bridge, this is a popular picnic spot and can be crowded in summer.

Cross the bridge and take the path downstream. Just after a gate the path divides. The top path goes towards Flash and the lower to Knar. Follow the lower path, which is closest to the river.

When the river is reached below Knar, do not cross it but take the track which bears left uphill and then turn right at a derelict barn. Follow this track uphill until you reach the ridge between the valley of the Dane and the small brook coming down from Flash. Turn right over a stile to follow the ridge of the hill. The paths are not well marked but, if you lose your way, you merely need to make for the hill ridge. Looking to the south, you should be able to see the Ramshaw Rocks and the Roaches on the skyline.

Follow the ridge downhill for about three quarters of a mile to the road below. Here turn right onto the road and then left along the riverbank path to the Gradbach car park. From the car park, first follow the road and then take the drive going down to Gradbach Mill which is now a Youth Hostel. As you approach the Mill, notice the mill leat on your right and the rather unusual horse trough on the left with its two stone seats. From the mill, take the path downstream to the footbridge over the Black Brook at its confluence with the Dane.

At the Black Brook, turn right to follow the river unless you wish to take a detour to see Lud's Church. This massive natural cleft in the rock is situated towards the top of the wood. It is reached by taking the path towards Swythamley and, when the top of the wood is reached at Castle Rock, taking the path which doubles back along the hillside.

Back at the river, the next three quarters of a mile is a most attractive walk through deciduous woodland with the river tumbling below. In places there are some quite deep gritstone gorges.

On coming out of the wood, the path climbs away from the river. When Back Dane Cottage is reached, the Dane is joined by the Clough Brook coming down from Wildboarclough. The path goes into woodland to take you down to Danebridge.

As you cross the bridge at Danebridge, look over the parapet at the riverbed below. It is easy to see why this was called Slider Ford before the building of the bridge. There is parking at the roadside at Danebridge and a pub, The Ship Inn, a little way up the hill.

It is difficult to imagine that this small road was once a major communications route, not just within the county, but also for traffic coming south from Scotland. Bonnie Prince Charlie's Army passed this way on the campaign of 1745.

After the bridge, take the road to the left which goes down to the trout farm. Pass the cottage and follow the path downstream through the fields for about a mile to the footbridge which you should cross. At the footbridge there are some quite substantial civil engineering works – retaining walls in the river and a weir. These were built to take a supply of water to the Caldon Canal six miles away when the canal was extended to Leek in 1797 (see 2.2 Caldon canal).

Follow the canal feeder for nearly two miles. It is a delightful walk with deciduous trees on either side of the Dane which look so attractive in autumn. The only drawback is that this path can be extremely muddy after rain.

You will recognise that you are approaching the A523 before you see it by the incessant traffic noise. This will remind you just how quiet the valley has been up to this point. Two fields before the A523, take the path across the fields down the road. (If it is too muddy to do so, carry on down the canal feeder and then turn right at the road). Cross the road and follow the path to and under the dismantled railway line.

There are two alternative ways of completing the walk:

either

a) At the dismantled railway line, climb the embankment and follow the track to the car park at the old station about a mile away at Rushton Spencer (next to the Knot Inn).

or

b) At the railway line, follow the path ahead towards The Cloud. This part of the walk is along the line of the Staffordshire Way, and you should follow the signpost with the "knot" insignia.

The path first bears right to follow the River Dane and then left away from the river up the deeply wooded ravine of Raven's Clough. (This stretch of the walk can be very muddy in wet weather).

You will come out of the ravine next to Raven's Clough Farm and then follow the farm road along the top edge of the ravine. When the road turns right, follow it for a short distance until you reach the footpath sign into the field to the left. Take this path across the fields to the road just below The Cloud.

Here bear left for a short distance before coming to the track which will take you to the top of The Cloud. On a clear day there are some magnificent views over the plain with Congleton in the foreground and the Welsh Hills in the distance.

If you look towards the south east, you should be able to see the jagged gritstone outline of The Roaches. To the right of The Roaches is the more rounded outline of Hen Cloud and, further to the right, high up on the skyline is the outline of the Mermaid Inn. This is the old drovers' inn which is the starting point of the Churnet Valley walk.

Places of interest in the Dane valley

3.1 The Cloud (Bosley Cloud)

The Cloud is derived from the Old English word Clud, meaning a rock or a hill. Owned by the National Trust, the Cloud provides spectacular views over the Cheshire plain some 600 feet below.

The shape of the Cloud leads to an unusual phenomenon in the Leek churchyard between June 20-22 (weather permitting). Here, the sun sets twice, first behind the Cloud and then, after briefly re-emerging, a second time over the Cheshire plain.

The view from Bosley Cloud

The road which skirts the Cloud on the south (about a mile away) is known as Earlsway, since it was used by the Earl of Chester when visiting his landholdings in the Peak District. (This is the same Earlsway seen at Waterfall Cross on the Hamps walk). One of the houses on this road is still known as Earlsway House.

Just north of this road is a well-preserved Burial Chamber of the bronze age period, the Bridestones.

3.2 Danebridge

The now minor road going through Danebridge was an important route in medieval times, being the main road between Leek and Macclesfield. The first mention of a bridge here is in 1357. Before that, there was a ford – Slider Ford. An inspection of the river bed with its flat inclined planes of shale confirms the appropriateness of the name.

Bonnie Prince Charlie's Army passed along this road in 1745 on its way to Derby and, until recently, the Ship Inn had a display of the relics of the period. The Inn sign is of the Nimrod in which Sir Philip Brocklehurst of Swythamley Hall went to the Antarctic with Shackleton.

The present bridge was rebuilt in 1869, when a cannon ball of the civil war period was found in the masonry.

3.3 Eagle and Child

Where the Allgreave to Flash road intersects the packhorse road coming up from Gradbach, there is a private dwelling with a stone carving over the door showing an eagle and a child. Between 1738 and 1919, this was the Eagle and Child Public House.

The significance of the insignia is that it is the coat of arms of Lord Derby who owns Crag Hall at Wildboarclough. One of the 14th century Earls of Derby had an illegitimate son of which his wife was unaware. The Earl hid the child in an eagle's nest on his estate and, when out walking with his wife, came across the child which had been "stolen" by the eagle. The family adopted the child.

3.4 Gradbach

The present mill building at Gradbach was erected in 1785 on the site of an earlier mill of 1640. Now a Youth Hostel, the mill has in its time processed flax and silk as well as being a sawmill, making carpets and evaporating "oker" riverwater to produce an orange/red dye for the textile industry. The mill at one time employed 200 people and was powered by a 38 ft waterwheel.

3.5 Hugbridge

Until 1620 when it burnt down, the bridge here was of wooden construction. Being on the boundary between Cheshire and Staffordshire, Cheshire promptly rebuilt its half of the bridge in stone. Staffordshire refused to accept any responsibility for the bridge saying that the local village should undertake the work.

3.6 Lud's Church

A deep cleft in the hillside at Back Forest above Gradbach, Lud's Church is named after the 14th century Walter de Lud Auk, the leader of a group of religious dissenters who used the "church" for their meetings. It is reputed to be the "Green Chapel" of the medieval poem "Sir Gawain and the Green Knight".

3.7 Swythamley Hall

The Hall stands on the site of a medieval grange of Dieulacresse Abbey at Leek. The original Hall, which was burnt down in 1813, featured as the "Green Knight's Castle" in the medieval poem "Sir Gawain and the Green Knight".

The Hall was rebuilt by the Brocklehurst family, using much stone from the original Hall. Sir Philip Brocklehurst travelled to the Antarctic with Shackleton in the Nimrod, the expedition being commemorated on the sign of the Ship Inn at Danebridge. Lt. Col Brocklehurst had a private zoo on the Roaches from which deer escaped and established themselves in the wild.

3.8 Wildboarclough

The last wild boar in England was supposedly killed at Wildboarclough in the 15th century. In 1800 George Palfreman of Monyash built a mill at Wildboarclough and engaged an apprentice, James Brindley, to install the equipment. The same James Brindley later became the famous canal engineer.

The mill, which at its peak employed 600, manufactured silk and later carpets. It was powered by a 30ft waterwheel. Palfreman built Crag Hall as his residence. After the mill closure this became the Earl of Derby's Shooting Lodge. Although the mill was demolished in the 1950s, the administrative building survives. At one time it housed the local sub-post office, and this was the largest sub-post office in England.

3.9 Wincle Grange

The first recorded mention of Wincle is as 'Winchal' in the 12th century. The grange was established in the 14th century as a sheep farm by the monks of Combermere Abbey in Cheshire.

Walk 4: River Derwent

Distances:

Total: 65 miles

Section 1: Howden Reservoir to Bamford: 9.6 miles

Section 2: Bamford to Baslow: 8.4 miles

Section 3: Baslow to Rowsley: 4.6 miles

Section 4: Rowsley to Cromford: 8.6 miles

Section 5: Cromford to Whatstandwell: 2.9 miles

Detour 1: Slippery Stones to Howden Edge: 10 miles

Detour 2: Calver and Eyam via Offerton and Highlow Halls: 6.2 miles

Detour 3: Stanage and Carl Wark: 7.7 miles

Detour 4: Curbar Gap and Baslow Edge: 3 miles

Detour 5: Cromford Canal to Wirksworth: 4 miles

Ordnance Survey maps: Outdoor Leisure 1, The Dark Peak; Outdoor Leisure 24, The White Peak. (A section of about 3 miles between Bamford and Leadmill is not covered by these 1:25,000 scale maps. Map 4.2 of this book should suffice for this area).

The Derwent is the major river of the Peak District, flowing from north to south through gritstone until the limestone is reached around Matlock. A series of millstone escarpments, or "edges", stretching some twenty miles, provides magnificent walking on the eastern side of the upper valley, with views not only over the Derwent, but also over the valleys and plateau beyond.

In earlier times, the river was a significant barrier to transport and the villages and towns were established at the river crossings. Originally fords, these crossings were replaced in medieval times by bridges. There is much evidence of former packhorse routes taking advantage of these river crossings and the gaps in the gritstone edges, and in a number of places the original pavings of these packhorse ways are still to be seen. The rights of way which have resulted from

The Derwent above the reservoirs

these ancient packhorse routes make the Derwent extremely accessible to the walker.

Chatsworth, the seat of the Dukes of Devonshire, is the most important historical building in the valley. There are several more modest but interesting Halls including North Lees, Offerton, Highlow, Eyam and Stoney Middleton. Eyam Hall, which has been continuously owned by a single family for over three centuries, is open to the public in the summer months, and is well worth a visit.

The section of the valley below Cromford is particularly rich in historical interest, with:

¤ Arkwright's Mill, the world's first powered cotton mill

¤ the Cromford canal, including its terminus and pumping station

¤ the Cromford and High Peak Railway

¤ the church at Wirksworth, which has one of the most important pieces of Anglo-Saxon stone carving in the country.

The word 'Derwent' is derived from the ancient British word meaning "abounding in oaks". While most of the natural oaks have long since been cleared, a few have still survived on the gritstone escarpments out of the reach of grazing animals. There is an important relict woodland in Padley Gorge.

Because of the length of the Derwent, and the very large number of places of interest in the valley, the walk is treated in a slightly different way from the walks in the other river valleys. A single continuous main walk down the valley is first described, followed by five detours. The detours could be treated as walks in their own right, using the section of the main walk along the river to turn them into circular walks.

The area around Matlock is omitted from the walks, overdevelopment during the 19th century limiting its attractiveness to the walker. Instead, the walk takes an interesting detour through Winster before rejoining the river at Cromford.

Wirksworth, on detour 5, is not strictly in the Derwent valley (it is on the River Ecclesbourne) but is included both because of the fine views over the Derwent in following the High Peak Trail and also because of the historical importance of the town.

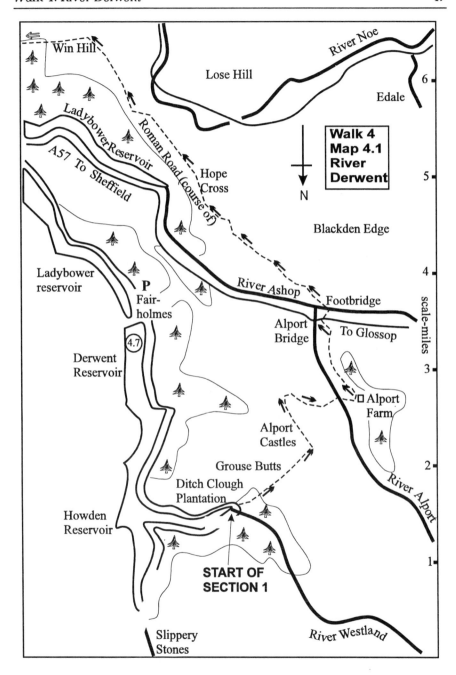

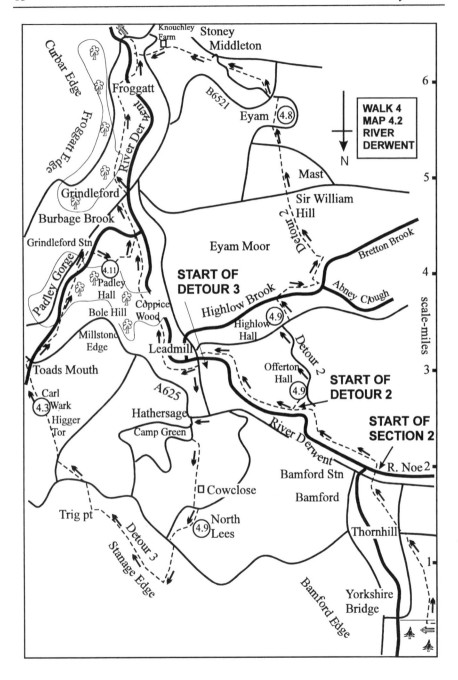

Knouchley Farm
Stoney Middleton
Curbar Edge
Froggatt
B6521
Eyam (4.8)
River Derwent
Froggatt Edge
Mast
Sir William Hill
Grindleford
Burbage Brook
Grindleford Stn
Eyam Moor
Bretton Brook
Padley Gorge
(4.11)
Padley Hall
START OF DETOUR 3
Highlow Brook
Abney Clough
Bole Hill
Coppice Wood
Millstone Edge
Highlow Hall
Detour 2
Leadmill
Toads Mouth
Offerton Hall
START OF DETOUR 2
Carl (4.3) Wark
A625
Higger Tor
Hathersage
River Derwent
START OF SECTION 2
Camp Green
R. Noe 2
Bamford Stn
Bamford
Cowclose
Trig pt
Detour 3
North (4.9) Lees
Thornhill
Stanage Edge
Bamford Edge
Yorkshire Bridge

WALK 4
MAP 4.2
RIVER
DERWENT
N

scale-miles
6
5
4
3
2
1

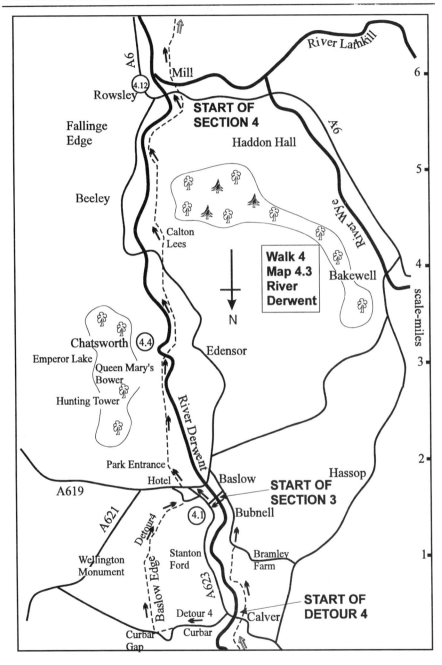

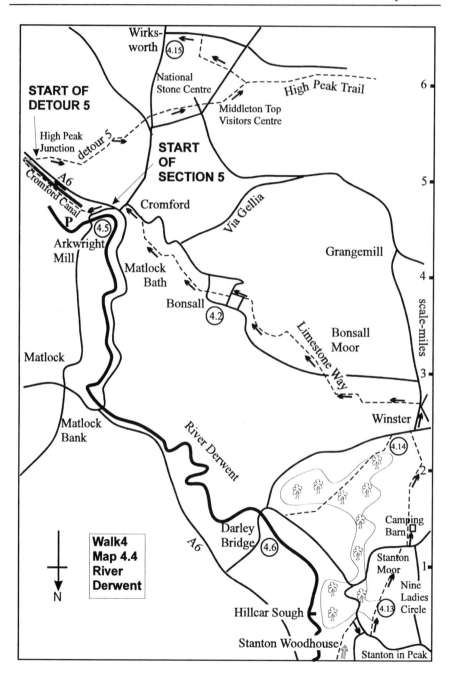

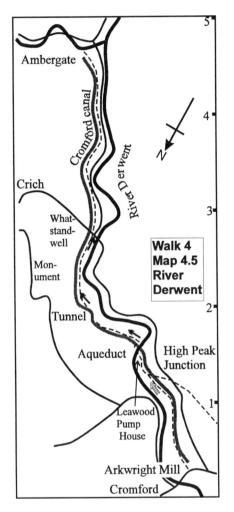

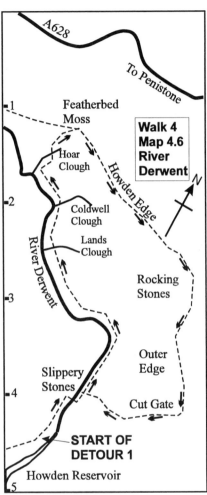

The Main Walk

Section 1: Howden Reservoir to Alport Castles and Bamford

Distance: 9.6 miles

Starting point: Ditch Clough Plantation SK 155928

Maps: 4.1 and 4.2

Although there are many paths around the Derwent Reservoirs, the conifer plantations and the sterile area above the water line make the walking rather dull. A much more interesting alternative to walking around the Reservoirs is to climb out of the Derwent Valley to the Alport Valley and then back to the Derwent Valley over Win Hill.

The starting point is at the western extremity of the Howden Reservoir, which may be reached by car during the week or, at the week-end, by a bus which runs frequently from Fairholmes car park.

The path climbs steeply through Ditch Clough Plantation, and then more gently past the grouse butts. It is worth looking back once above the plantation. There are good views of the Howden Reservoir and, silhouetted against the skyline, are Howden Edge and Outer Edge.

Just over a mile and after a climb of some 700 feet from the Howden Reservoir, the Alport Castles are reached (see 1.1, Ashop Walk). Some caution is required, for ahead there is a precipitous drop of several hundred feet.

The path follows the rim of the Castles towards the south east, before going down the eastern side of the landslip. Follow the path down to the River Alport, pass Alport Farm and then proceed down the valley to Alport Bridge. Although Alport Castles is the most impressive of the landslips, a careful inspection of the valley sides shows numerous smaller landslips.

Alport Castles

When Alport Bridge is reached, cross the road. Descend to the river and cross the footbridge. Just upstream of the footbridge you will see a concrete structure. This diverts water from the Ashop into a feeder which carries it through the hills to the Derwent Reservoir. The River Alport is similarly diverted and, as a result, the riverbed below Alport Bridge is sometimes dry.

After the footbridge, the path climbs steadily some 400 feet towards the south east, following an old packhorse way to Yorkshire bridge. About two miles after leaving Alport Bridge, the path reaches a saddle between the Derwent and the Noe. Here, you are on the old Roman Road from Glossop to Navio. The stone guide post, Hope Cross, is dated 1737, but is of much earlier origin. During the Second World War, when there was the threat of invasion, the Cross was disassembled and buried. On re-erection it was incorrectly re-assembled, so you should disregard its directions.

In about two miles from Hope Cross, the summit of Win Hill is reached. The summit, Winhill Pike, is very distinctive. There are extensive panoramic views from the Pike over several valleys and, looking back, over most of the route you have followed since leaving the Howden Reservoir.

From the top of Win Hill, take the path to the east which, after a stile, descends towards Yorkshire Bridge. The path enters a wood and, when a fence is reached, turns right to follow the contour of the hill. Follow the old packhorse road until it begins to bear right. Here you take a path to the left which descends towards Thornhill.

On reaching Thornhill, turn left when the road is reached, and proceed to the junction between this road and the road to Yorkshire Bridge (this is the main junction of the village). About 100 yards downhill from this junction, there is a path leading off to the left (just after a gate marked Barleylands). Take this path and follow a hollow-way down to meet a track. Turn left here to go in front of a mansion which a stone plaque indicating that it was the home of The Derwent Valley Water Board. Turn right here, follow the hedge line down the field and go under the railway track.

Cross the main road, to bring you to the River Noe Bridge just above the confluence with the Derwent. This completes this section of the walk.

Section 2: Bamford to Baslow

Distance: 8.4 miles

Starting point: Bridge over the Noe near Bamford SK 203827

Maps: 4.2 and 4.3

From the bridge, the path goes into the field on the left. The entrance is somewhat concealed, and may not be obvious until you are level with it. After the field, the path crosses rather undulating ground, with fairly precipitous drops to the river below. The fence is in disrepair, and care should be taken in wet weather, when the path is likely to be slippery.

At the end of the undulating section, the river leaves the hillside. The path drops to the alluvial plain where it follows the river which is running on bedrock typically ten to fifteen feet below.

Although there are some old hedge divisions across the field, these have been allowed to fall into disrepair to produce a single field approximately half a mile in length.

When the river next meets the hillside, there is a track ahead to Offerton Hall. Ignore this, taking the footbridge over a stream, followed by some steps down to the riverbank.

In a short distance, there is a crossing of two paths. To your left, there are stepping stones leading to Hathersage, and the path to the right is the start of detour 2 described later. Even though you are taking the path down the riverbank, it is worth going onto the stones to get a view up and down the river. These stepping stones are of considerable antiquity, and are mentioned in a 16th century record.

As you proceed ahead, the views are of Hathersage and the Edges whilst, behind, Winhill Pike can still be seen. Follow the path along the riverbank until the river meets the hillside again.

Because the River Derwent is both heavily wooded and normally running on bedrock below the alluvial plain, it is rarely possible to see riverwater from the hillside above. The next half mile or so is an exception, since it flows directly towards Millstone Edge. From the Edges above Hathersage, it is this stretch of the river which may be seen glistening below.

A bridge is reached at Leadmill which you cross. The road ahead to Hathersage is the start of detour 3, but the main walk bears right, next to the bridge, towards Harper Lees.

Until the 16th century, lead was smelted on west facing hilltops, using the winds to create a draft. In the 16th century, a new process was developed which used water-powered bellows. It was then that a smelter was established at Leadmill (which had previously been called Hazelford). Later still, a more advanced cupola smelting technique was developed and smelting migrated from Leadmill to Hathersage. The old mill leat of the smelter can be seen between the path and the river.

After Harper Lees you will come to Coppice Wood. In common with Bole Hill above, Coppice Wood has a very large population of ants and, when they are active, this is not a place to sit down and enjoy your sandwiches.

Although out of sight, the Manchester to Sheffield railway is running very close at hand, so don't be surprised to hear the occasional train.

The Burbage Brook is reached at the end of the second field after leaving Coppice Wood, and here detour 3 rejoins the main walk. Two more fields bring you to Grindleford.

At Grindleford, follow the road down to the river and enter the field just before the bridge. Take the path diagonally across the field towards the corner of the woods. (The path down the riverbank at the bridge is a cul-de-sac).

The path ahead to Froggatt is a medieval packhorse route as evidenced by the extensive lengths of stone flags. Froggatt is a delightful village. Notice the name of the road by which the walk enters the village. Hollowgate is nearly always an indication of an old packhorse way.

Follow the road to and across the bridge. Here the river is deep and slow moving, suggesting a weir downstream. The weir is met just after the next bridge and the path follows the millstream (or goit) from the weir to the mill at Calver. Calver Mill was built by Arkwright in 1803 and is still in use (manufacturing stainless steel). It was used as the set for the film "Colditz".

The starting point for detour 4 to Baslow Edge is just over the old bridge at Calver. For the main walk, take the path which goes under the modern bridge and passes a housing estate before coming out into the fields.

The path leaves the riverbank when it enters a small wood. On leaving this wood, a building is seen on the opposite bank which is Stanton Ford. In medieval times, this was an important ford taking traffic between the Derwent and the Wye, and the line of the route may still be seen in the field boundaries. This is best seen looking down on the river from Baslow Edge, and is noted on that part of detour 4.

Turn left when a minor road is met, to go through the attractive village of Bubnell on your way to Baslow. In crossing the medieval bridge into Baslow, notice the unusual guardhouse on the bridge. In medieval times, the male population of many of these villages was required to take turns as night watchmen.

Turn right onto the A623, to come to the church.

Section 3: Baslow-Rowsley

Distance: 4.6 miles

Starting point: Baslow Church SK 252723

Map: 4.3

From Baslow church, follow the main road for perhaps three hundred yards, ignoring the A619 turning (to Bakewell). Just after the entrance to a caravan site, and before the Cavendish Hotel, take the path which leads behind the hotel. After a small bridge, the path joins another and proceeds to the entrance to the Chatsworth Estate.

A notice board at the entrance gives some details of the park, including the fact that some of the oak trees are a thousand years old, being remnants of the western edge of the Sherwood Forest.

After passing a walled garden and a cricket field, the panorama could have been painted by Turner:

¤ a Palladian house in the middle distance with fountain behind

¤ The Elizabethan Hunting Tower on the hillside

¤ the river flowing to the right

¤ sheep on the meadows (if in residence)

The building on the right by the bridge is Queen Mary's Bower, named after Mary Queen of Scots who was held captive at Chatsworth on several occasions between 1570 and 1581.

Both the House and Gardens are well worth a visit. A minimum of half a day is needed to do full justice to a visit to Chatsworth but, if you are really pressed for time, an hour in each will give a first impression.

To leave Chatsworth, cross the bridge next to Queen Mary's Bower and take the path down the river. At the southern end of the Estate, cross the road and take the path into and through the car park. Pass the Garden Centre and the Estate Sawmill towards the hamlet of Calton Lees. Immediately after Calton Lees House, a path bears left and descends to the river meadow.

After some twenty miles of Edges on the eastern side of the valley, you are now entering more rolling countryside. Fallinge Edge is the last of the gritstone Edges. Notice how, even after afforestation and clearing of the wood crop, there is still evidence on the hillside of the scars caused by former packhorse routes.

As you proceed down the valley, some cottages come into view perched on the opposite hillside above the river. Rowsley was once an important railway junction and these were railway workers' cottages.

The natural route for the railway to take after Rowsley was up the Derwent valley through Chatsworth, but the Duke would never allow this. Instead, the railway had to take the much more difficult line up the river Wye.

The path joins and follows the river to Rowsley. After passing under the old railway bridge, turn left at the minor road which goes down to the A6.

The Peacock Hotel is on the corner of the main road. Notice the stone peacock over the main entrance. The hotel was originally the Dower House for Haddon Hall, and the peacock was the family crest of the Manners family of Haddon.

Section 4: Rowsley to Cromford

Distance: 8.6 miles

Starting point: Peacock Hotel, Rowsley SK 257659

Maps: 4.3 and 4.4

From the Peacock Hotel, cross the A6 into School Lane. In a short distance, the bridge over the River Wye is reached (the junction with the river Derwent is not far downstream). The mill just upstream on the River Wye is worth a visit.

After crossing the Wye, the road bears right but a more minor road proceeds ahead. Take this minor road, climbing gently through a wood until Stanton Woodhouse and its associated farm is reached.

Stanton Woodhouse was the 16th century Shooting Lodge of the Duke of Rutland and was the residence of the Duke when Haddon Hall was being renovated earlier this century. Take the path to the right of Stanton Woodhouse which passes between the house and the farmhouse.

Climbing upward, there are good views up and down the Derwent.

When a minor road coming up from the valley bottom is reached, turn right and follow it as it climbs round the hillside, ignoring the minor road to the right. A sign to the left points the way to the Bronze Age Nine Ladies Circle. Some comments scribbled on the signpost suggest the frustration of previous visitors who have taken the path but been unable to find the Circle!

To get to the Circle, climb upwards into the wood keeping close to its right-hand edge. For a distance follow a barbed wire fence. A break in the fence eventually allows direct access to the Circle.

After viewing the Circle, rejoin the footpath and proceed along Stanton Moor Edge. A memorial to Earl Grey's part in the 1832 Reform Act is just down the Edge followed by a stone with the inscription EIN 1831 and some footholes to allow it to be climbed.

The path down the Edge gives excellent views over the valley below. The area appears not be grazed and, as a result, the bilberry bushes are tall and can be very rewarding in early July.

When a minor road is reached, turn right and then almost immediately left past a Camping Barn, Barn Farm. Cross another path and then a "green" lane which was a drove road to Darley Bridge. Winster is seen ahead when you reach a valley. Take the path down to the bottom of the valley and then up into Winster. The path up into Winster is a very heavily worn flagged path, indicating a well-used packhorse way.

Winster is an architectural gem with some sixty listed buildings. Many of these reflect Winster's earlier prosperity as an important market town. The most prominent building is the Market House built in 1700; see photograph on the next page.

From Winster, it is possible to walk across the fields to Darley Dale bridge, passing a number of lead spoil heaps on the way. The main walk however is over Bonsall Moor to Bonsall and Cromford. Take West Bank, the road which climbs steeply southwards out of Winster to the Miners Standard Inn. If you need an excuse for refreshment, this Inn has an interesting collection of lead mining memorabilia, and the landlord is very knowledgeable on mining and caving matters.

The Market House, Winster

At the Inn, two roads meet obliquely. Take the left fork towards Grangemill. Almost immediately, there is a sign to the left onto the Limestone Way, a walk between Matlock and Castleton which is also used on the Lathkill Walk in the vicinity of Youlgreave.

Follow the Limestone Way towards Bonsall. Just above Winster there is an unusual wooden seat by the side of the path which, appropriately for this area, has lead straps. The path climbs over the edge of Bonsall Moor, a large number of mounds indicating former lead mining activity. The scenery is most attractive; undulating limestone country with small fields and limestone walls.

The Limestone Way enters Bonsall past Hollies Farm. Notice just after the farm that the wall on the left of the road has a mixture of stone types – limestone, magnesian limestone, gritstone and basalt, indicating a complex geology in this area.

At the end of the lane, a T-junction is reached. The Limestone Way takes the path almost directly ahead which first passes some houses and then descends steeply between stone walls to the centre of Bonsall where there is an impressive market cross surrounded by thirteen concentric steps.

From the cross take the small road which climbs up past the church. At Town End Farm the road terminates, but a footpath proceeds ahead. Follow this, skirting around a large quarry, before descending to Cromford (ignore the road to your right which descends into the quarry). On entering Cromford you will pass two small reservoirs, built to provide a water supply for downstream mills. When the T-junction is reached, turn left. On your left is the Greyhound Inn, a Coaching Inn built by Sir Richard Arkwright.

In a couple of hundred yards, the busy A6 is reached. Take the small road almost directly across the A6 towards the river. On the left you will pass the Arkwright Mill, which was the first cotton mill to use water power. The road goes under a cast iron structure with the date 1821 inscribed. This was bringing a supply of water to an overshot wheel in the mill. The mill is now a museum.

Section 5: Cromford to Whatstandwell

Distance: 2.9 miles

Starting point: Cromford canal terminus SK 300570

Map: 4.5

Just down the road from the Arkwright Mill is the terminus of the Cromford canal. From the entrance to the terminus you can see the 15th century bridge over the river, and you may care to go down and have a look at it since it has a number of interesting features mentioned in 4.5.

From the canal terminus, follow the towpath and, in about a mile, High Peak Junction is reached. This is the junction of the Cromford canal and the 33 mile railway which goes across the Peak District to Whaley Bridge. (Detour 5 to Wirksworth via the High Peak Tail starts here). At the Junction are warehouses and transshipment facilities and a workshop where the locomotives were assembled and maintained.

About a quarter of a mile after High Peak Junction, the Lea Wood Pumping Station is reached. This had the capacity to pump four tons of water from the river into the canal with each stroke of its engine and is still occasionally steamed.

Just after the Pumping Station, an aqueduct takes the canal over the river and you should cross the small bridge to proceed down the other bank of the canal. The canal towpath now proceeds through very pleasant wooded scenery down the valley. Although the busy A6 is running parallel to the canal, and is not very far away, it is out of sight and is unobstrusive.

At one point, the canal and the towpath pass through a short tunnel. On emerging, you will see a monument to the Sherwood Foresters directly ahead on the hilltop.

At Whatstandwell, there is a limited amount of parking by the canal and there is a pub.

The Detours

Detour 1: Slippery stones-Howden Edge

Distance: 10 miles

Starting point: Top Car Park, Howden Reservoir SK 168938

Map: 4.6

During the week, cars have access to the length of the reservoirs. At weekends, cars may only be taken as far as Fairholmes. From Fairholmes, a half hourly bus service gives access to the head of the reservoirs.

From the car park near the head of Howden Reservoir, take the path up river. In just under a mile, the packhorse bridge at Slippery Stones is reached. Cross the bridge, and in a short distance the path divides. The way to the right is the old packhorse route called Cut Gate, and is the route by which you will be returning later. For the moment, take the path up the valley. For the next two miles there is an easy walk along a sandstone track.

You have left now behind the rather artificial looking conifer plantations of the reservoirs. The vegetation, whilst somewhat sparse, is that which is natural to the Upper Derwent; Oak, Ash, Birch and Bilberry. The area is grazed, and the trees tend to be limited to the crevices which the sheep cannot reach.

The good sandstone track gives way to a moorland path at Lands Clough. The path ahead has a tendency to be boggy after heavy rain.

At Hoar Clough (the second stream on the right-hand bank after Lands Clough), the path turns right up the clough, climbing for about another half a mile until the summit is reached at the top of Featherbed Moss. The path joining from the west is from Bleaklow.

The very gentle convexity of the hilltops means that the Etherow and the Don valleys beyond may only be seen in the distance. The Holme Moss TV mast should be visible to the north.

You have now climbed some 800 feet since leaving the reservoirs and are at the lowest altitude where the Cloudberry may be seen. Identified by its coarse green foliage, single white flower and red-coloured fruit, the Cloudberry, grows in abundance on the wetter moorland beside the path.

Take the path to the east and follow the high ground. For the next couple of miles the path ahead is featureless which makes navigation surprisingly difficult. The coarse grass, whilst only sparse, is tall enough to obscure the path more than thirty yards ahead. With no middle distance markers, eyes have to be kept firmly on the path if retracing of steps is to be avoided.

Where small streams run off the moor, they cut surprisingly deep incisions into the peat. These eroded areas can be tricky to cross after rain which converts the exposed peat to a bog.

Navigation problems are eased when a line of wooden stakes is reached. In addition to the wooden stakes, there are some interesting stone waymarkers displaying a deeply cut letter B. This was the mark of the early 18th century surveyor who, after an Act of 1702, was required to signpost all cross roads in his area of responsibility.

The path also passes a number of glacial erratics which have been weathered into interesting shapes. To the east, silhouetted against the Derwent Valley, are the Rocking Stones. Even from a distance these look precariously balanced.

The highest point on the walk is reached at the trig point on Outer Edge, and, in just under a mile, Cut Gate, the pack horse route seen just above Slippery Stones, is reached.

Take the path to the right down Cut Gate and descend towards the Howden Reservoir. For the first mile the descent is gentle but, when the disused quarries are reached just before Slippery Stones, the path steepens and some care is required.

Detour 2: Calver and Eyam, via Offerton and Highlow Halls.

Distance: 6.2 miles

Starting point: River Derwent stepping stones SK 217815

Map: 4.2

Take the path from the stepping stones over the River Derwent towards Offerton Hall. The half mile track through the fields is smooth and well-graded and has obviously been much used over the centuries.

At the minor road there are two fine 17th century buildings, the one on the left being Offerton Hall. Follow the road which climbs behind the Hall. From this road there are fine views over the other side of the valley.

In just under a mile from Offerton Hall, Highlow Hall, another fine 17th century Hall, is reached at the T-junction with the road coming up from Leadmill.

Immediately to the west of Highlow Hall, take the path through the gate (not signposted) which skirts the Hall and descends to Highlow Brook. Cross the brook, and take the path which follows the brook upstream. Sessile oak, ash and birch cluster round the brook bottom.

The path divides at the junction of Abney Clough and Bretton Clough. Take the path to the left which shortly turns back on itself as it climbs to higher ground. As height is gained, there are good views up Bretton Brook towards Camphill, the home of the Derbyshire Gliding Club.

Just before reaching a small wood, climb the stile across a wall. Here the path divides into three, each of which could be taken to reach Eyam. Take the middle path.

When the cairn on the hilltop is reached, there are fine views to the east and north. The flatness of the hilltop gives less interesting views to the south.

Cross two small roads and bear left to skirt a small plantation. The path now descends steeply, crossing a road and a field before coming to a stile. Over the stile, a path leads to the churchyard in the centre of Eyam. In passing through the churchyard, you will see one of the finest Anglo-Saxon Crosses in the Peak District. The church has many associations with the plague period of 1665/6. If you have the time, Eyam Hall, which is to the right, is well worth a visit.

After the church, take the road to the left. Cross the Square into the small road called Lydgate. There is a notice on the wall explaining its history.

When Lydgate divides, take the path ahead into the fields. These fields are pockmarked with small mine spoil heaps.

When you come to a large boundary stone, notice that it has small indentations. During the plague year of 1665/6, when Eyam isolated itself, stones at the periphery of the village such as this were used as supply points for the villagers. Provisions were left here, and money was left in the vinegar filled indentations. This was in the mistaken belief that vinegar was a disinfectant.

As you enter Stoney Middleton, notice the small octagonal building below the path on the main road. This was originally a toll house, and is now the Fish and Chips shop. Do not join the main road, but keep to the old road which runs parallel to it towards the church.

The church is most unusual, being octagonal and having pews which face each other. Take the road to the left round the church. Here is the so called "Roman Baths", making use of a 63° F spring. (There is no evidence of this spring having any association with the Roman occupation and the baths date from the late medieval period).

After passing the 17th century Hall on the right, the path passes into the meadows. When the path divides, take the left fork which climbs the hill before passing behind Knouchley Farm. Cross the Grindleford to Calver Road and proceed down the field to rejoin the main walk at the river's edge just above Calver.

Detour 3: Stanage Edge and Carl Wark (taking in Hathersage, North Lees, Padley Gorge and Padley Chapel)

Distance: 7.7 miles

Starting point: Leadmill bridge SK 233806

Map: 4.2

This detour leaves the main walk at Leadmill Bridge. Follow the road up into Hathersage. On meeting the A625, the 16th century George Inn faces you. When Charlotte Bronte stayed in Hathersage, the landlord of the Inn was a Mr Morton. Bronte named the village in Jayne Eyre after him.

Turn right down the A625 and follow it through the village. Turn left into School Road. The pub on this road is called the Scotsman's Pack Inn, a reference to its former clientele. At the Scotsman's Pack, take the road to the left which climbs steeply to the church.

There is much to see in and around the church, including

¤ some fine brasses of the Eyre family in the church sanctuary

¤ Little John's grave in the churchyard

¤ the Vicarage to the west of the church where Charlotte Bronte stayed

¤ a well-preserved fortification on Camp Green to the east of the church which is dated from around AD850 and is said to have been built by the Vikings.

The path to Stanage starts from the north eastern corner of the churchyard. After crossing a small brook it climbs the fields. When the path divides, take the right fork towards Cowclose Farm.

A small road leading up to Stanage is met after Cowclose. Turn

Abandoned millstones below Millstone Edge.

left here and then right up the drive to North Lees. This fine hall, built in 1596, was one of the numerous Eyre houses and was the inspiration for Thornfield Hall in Jane Eyre. It is now a farm and a guest house.

Leaving North Lees, the path climbs to the road skirting the bottom edge of Stanage which it joins next to a public convenience. Turn left onto the road and then right into the car park. A path up to Stanage Edge leaves this car park. In places it is flagged, a relic of the time when this was a packhorse route which crossed the Derwent at Leadmill on its way to Sheffield.

From the top of the Edge there are extensive views, not only over Hathersage and the Derwent, but also of Edale and Kinder Scout.

Follow the path along the top of Stanage Edge towards the south east for about a mile. Just before a trig point, a path leads down to the road coming up from Hathersage. There are a number of abandoned millstones here, lying between the path and the gritstone edge. Cross the road and then another road before climbing up onto the rocky outcrop of Higger Tor. Descend from Higger Tor towards the ancient fort of Carl Wark, about a quarter of a mile to the south.

From Carl Wark, the path descends to cross the Burbage Brook. (Just to the west of the point where the Burbage Brook goes under the road there is a gritstone outcrop named Toad's Mouth which bears an uncanny resemblance to a toad). Cross the A625 and follow the Burbage Brook downstream, first across the open grassland, and then into Padley Gorge. (If you are interested in seeing a large number of abandoned millstones, these may be found at SK 248800 beside the track which leads down to Bole Hill from Millstone Edge – just under a mile to the west of the Toads Mouth).

The walk through Padley Gorge is most pleasant with the brook tumbling over gritstone boulders in a relict hardwood forest. This must have been the typical woodland in the Derwent valley before clearance by Neolithic man. The hardwood trees support a large population of insects and, as a result, attract birds which are rarely seen in the open valley below.

At the bottom of the gorge there is a path from the main road to the railway station. Take this, crossing the brook at the old water mill. The marshalling yard looks rather large for a country village, but it must be remembered that over a million tons of rock was taken out of Bole Hill Quarry above and transported by train to build the Derwent Reservoirs.

After the station, Padley Chapel is reached with its connections with the Padley Martyrs. Cross the railway line and take the path across the fields to rejoin the main walk at the confluence of the Burbage Brook and the Derwent.

Detour 4: Curbar Gap and Baslow Edge

Distance: 3 miles

Starting point: Old bridge, Calver SK 247745

Map: 4.3

From the old bridge over the Derwent at Calver, climb the steep hill to the village of Curbar above. The road continues to climb after Curbar. Just before reaching Curbar Gap, the road bears left. A path provides a short cut directly to the gap.

At the crest of the hill, turn right onto Baslow Edge. From here you should have splendid views up and down the Derwent and over to the Wye and Lathkill valleys. (If you look carefully you should just be able to make out the angular Fin Cop hill fort on the Wye above Monsal Head). To the east, on the gritstone plateau, there were extensive settlements in the Bronze Age period. Curbar Gap must have been used as a communication route between the Derwent and the Wye right back into prehistory.

In walking down Baslow Edge, you should be able to see the line of a medieval communication route between the two rivers. On the west bank of the river, a small road is seen going down to a single dwelling at the river (Stanton Ford). On the opposite bank, there is no corresponding road immediately adjacent to the river, but its line can be seen further up the field at Bramley Farm. This was the line of a medieval road from Curbar Gap to Tideswell on the Wye which crossed the Derwent at Stanton Ford. Unlike so many fords of the Derwent, for some reason this ford was never upgraded to a bridge. Part of the line of this medieval route has been incorporated into modern roads and other parts have been lost.

When you reach the end of Baslow Edge you will have a good view down the valley over Chatsworth and, if it is working, the fountain behind. To your left is the monument to Wellington erected in 1866 and a large glacial erratic, the Eagle Stone.

Detour 5: Cromford Canal to Wirksworth

Distance: 4 miles

Starting point: High Peak Junction SK 313560

Map: 4.4

This detour follows the High Peak Trail from the junction with the Cromford canal. At the junction are the wharves for the transshipment of goods, and the railway workshops in which the locomotives were built and maintained.

Before the introduction of locomotives, the wagons were pulled for most of the distance between Cromford and Whaley Bridge by horse. The part you will be walking was too steep for this. The wagons had to be pulled up the inclines by stationary engines.

The first engine house (empty) is seen about a mile after the junction. Just past this engine house, there is an excellent panoramic view over the Derwent valley below, with Cromford in the foreground and the limestone gorge at Matlock behind.

Just over a mile beyond this first engine house, the National Stone Centre is on the left of the trail. After a further steep incline of about half a mile, the Visitor Centre at Middleton Top is reached. Here, the splendid beam engine of 1829 may be viewed.

From the Visitor Centre follow the High Peak Trail for a short distance until a quarry road is reached. Turn left here and then almost immediately right into the fields. Cross the road and fields until you come to the edge of a large limestone quarry. Turn right to skirt the quarry and, when a minor road is reached, bear left to descend to Wirksworth. In its heyday, Wirksworth was a town of some importance, as may be judged by looking at its buildings. The church in particular is worth a visit. It houses one of the most important Anglo-Saxon sculptures in the country.

Places of interest in the Derwent valley

4.1 Baslow

Baslow is one of the villages which grew up at a fording point of the Derwent. A bridge is first recorded in 1500, when there is mention of it being subjected to excessive weights due to the transport of millstones. The present bridge was built in 1609, and includes a guardhouse which is only three feet six inches high. The reason for this lack of headroom was that the road surface was later raised.

The nearby St Anne's Church has a number of unusual features including

¤ a lead plaque in the porch bearing the outline of a pointed shoe

¤ a clockface which has VICTORIA1897 in place of the normal numerals

¤ a whip inside the church to drive out stray dogs.

Bronze Age stock enclosures have been found above the village, on Gardom's Edge. Farming would have been abandoned on the Edge in the first millennium BC, when a climatic deterioration made much of the high land on the eastern side of the Derwent valley unusable.

On Baslow Edge there is a monument to Wellington erected in 1866. Nearby there is a large glacial erratic, known as the Eagle Stone.

4.2 Bonsall

Bonsall is a long linear village with a fall of some 400 feet from one end of the village to the other. Lead mining and textiles were previously the mainstays of the economy. St James' Church was built in the 13th century and the main square has a magnificent market cross with 13 concentric stone steps.

Via Gellia, a two mile road built by Philip Gell of Hopton in 1791, is at the bottom of the village. The Gells claim an ancestry back to the Roman occupation of Britain and there are some fine monuments to the family in Wirksworth church. Today, the Gells are perhaps best-known for a derivative of their name. Viyella, a type of cloth, was first manufactured at the Hollins Mill and took the name of the road.

Half way down the Via Gellia is probably the only house in Britain built of Tufa (see the Introduction for a description of Tufa).

4.3 Carl Wark

Carl Wark is a two acre site with a wall of large Millstone Blocks and an earth rampart. Originally thought to be of the Iron Age, current thinking is that it is more likely to be post-Roman. Carl Wark and the adjacent Higger Tor are good vantage points for viewing the Derwent valley below.

4.4 Chatsworth, "The Palace of the Peak"

The first Palace at Chatsworth was built by Sir William and Lady Cavendish (Bess of Hardwick). Mary Queen of Scots was a prisoner of Bess of Hardwick's fourth husband, the Earl of Shrewsbury, and spent much time at Chatsworth between 1570 and 1581. Apart from Queen Mary's Bower, which is believed to date from that time, the only other remnant of the Elizabethan Chatsworth is the Hunting Tower.

The present house was built by the first Duke of Devonshire between 1678 and 1707. He is reputed to have fallen out with his architect and designed the house himself. The landscaping is by Capability Brown.

The Emperor Fountain in the gardens is capable of 290 feet, the second highest fountain in Europe, and is made possible by a water supply from the Emperor Lake on the hillside.

Over the centuries, Chatsworth has successfully resisted the intrusions of the outside world. The 6th Duke moved the village of Edensor out of sight of Chatsworth to its present position, and the railway was refused access to Chatsworth both from the north and the south. The London to Manchester Railway had to take the difficult line up the Wye valley, and the line from Manchester through the Edale valley had to proceed eastwards through the three mile Totley tunnel after reaching Grindleford.

4.5 Cromford

Inspection of the 15th century bridge over the river shows that it has been subsequently widened. There are the ruined remains of a medieval chapel at the southern side of the bridge. (This would have been destroyed at the Dissolution of the Monasteries). Next to the chapel, and in better repair, is an 18th century "fishing temple" with the inscription "Piscatoribus Sacrum" – sacred to fishermen. An inscription on the parapet of the bridge records an incident when a Benjamin Hayward leapt into the river on his horse and survived a fall of some twenty feet!

The first "sough" in the Peak District to drain a lead mine was built at Cromford by the Dutchman Vermuyden in 1629-36. It was the water from this sough which attracted Arkwright to come to Cromford to build the world's first powered spinning mill in 1771. He built his second mill in 1783, and subsequently many others in the Peak District. The first mill eventually failed when, in 1840, the lowering of the water table in the mines removed the source of the water. In addition to his mills, Arkwright built many other buildings in Cromford including

¤ North Street for his workers (named after the then Prime Minister)

¤ the Greyhound Inn, a Coaching Inn

¤ Willersley Castle, a residence for himself which he never lived to occupy

¤ the church.

Close to the Arkwright Mill is the terminus of the Cromford Canal which was opened in 1794 to transport lead ore, stone and cotton. About a mile down the canal is the Lea Wood Pump House. This was designed to transfer 4 tons of water into the canal from the river at each stroke of the engine. The pump is still occasionally steamed.

Between Cromford and the Pump House is the terminus of the Cromford and High Peak Railway, opened in 1830 to carry goods to the High Peak Canal at Whaley Bridge 33 miles away. Stationary engines pulled the wagons up the steep inclines to the plateau above where they were drawn by horse until 1840. The line closed in 1960 and has now been converted into a long distance walk. The Middleton Top Engine house, with its beam engine of 1829, is open to the public.

4.6 Darley Dale

There has been a bridge over the Derwent at Darley Dale since the 15th century. Just to the west of the bridge, at Mill Close, was the largest lead mine in Britain. The mine only closed in 1938 when a water course flooded the mine workings. The site is now a factory for the reprocessing of lead batteries. It is the only remnant of an industry which dominated the economy of the Peak District for centuries.

The church of St Helens was built in the 12th century and there is a yew tree in the churchyard with a circumference of 33 feet. Estimates of the age of the yew range from 1000 to 2000 years. The implication of the greater age is that the church must have been built on a previously pagan site.

To the north of Darley Dale, the Hillcar Sough (shown on map 4.4) drains the Alport mines into the Derwent. With a total length of 4 miles, the sough took some 21 years to build. The enormous cost of the undertaking was recovered by a levy on all lead mined below a certain level.

4.7 The Derwent Reservoirs

In 1899, the Derwent Valley Water Board was set up to build reservoirs in the Derwent and Ashop valleys to supply Nottingham, Leicester and Sheffield.

The Howden Reservoir with a capacity of 1980 million gallons was the first to be built (1901-1912), followed by the Derwent with a capacity of 2120 gallons (1902-1916). A temporary town of almost 1000 was set up at Birchinlee to house the construction workers and their families.

The one and a quarter million tons of stone needed to build the two reservoirs was taken from the Bole Hill quarries, above Hathersage, and transported from Grindleford to Bamford by train.

To augment the water supply to the Derwent basin, the waters from the Ashop and Alport were diverted in 1930, and taken by tunnel through the hills. The entry point for this water is seen at the bottom end of the Derwent on the western bank.

The Ladybower Reservoir, which has a capacity of 6300 million gallons, was built between 1935 and 1943 with water later being diverted from the Noe and Peakshole Water and transported through Win Hill.

The villages of Derwent and Ashopton were inundated by the Ladybower Reservoir. The medieval packhorse bridge at Derwent was dismantled in 1933 and rebuilt at Slippery Stones at the head of the Howden Reservoir in 1959.

The Derwent was used by RAF 617 squadron when practising for the dam buster raids over Germany and later, for the filming of the raid. The valley is today frequently used for low flying practice.

There are many walks around the banks of the reservoirs, and there is vehicular access along the western bank during the week. At weekends, cars are restricted to the lower end of the reservoirs as far as Fairholmes. There is however a regular bus service from Fairholmes to the top of Howden. Cycles may be hired at Fairholmes.

4.8 Eyam

Eyam is famous for its self-sacrifice in the plague year of 1665/6, when it voluntarily isolated itself from the outside world. 259 of the population of 350 died, including the wife of Vicar Mompesson who organised the isolation.

In the 13th century church is the Mompesson chair and the plague record. The finest Saxon cross in the Peak District is in the churchyard.

The 17th century Eyam Hall is open to the public in the summer months.

4.9 Eyre Halls

The Eyres were one of the most prominent landowners in the Derwent valley, the family having come to England with William the Conqueror. Separate mention is made of their 14th century Hall at Padley (4.11) and their brasses in Hathersage Church (4.10).

In the 17th century, Robert Eyre of Highlow Hall is said to have installed his seven sons in Halls which were in sight of each other – Offerton, Upper and Nether Shatton, Crookshill, North Lees, Moorseats and Hazelford.

Highlow Hall is said to be haunted.

4.10 Hathersage

The town of Hathersage is aptly named, being a derivative of "Heathers Edge". Although a bustling tourist town today, Hathersage has a strong industrial history in metal working (particularly needlemaking), quarrying, both for construction stone and millstones (many of which may be seen abandoned below Millstone Edge) and lead smelting.

Robin Hood's giant companion, Little John, is by legend a son of the town, being born John Nailor and buried in the churchyard. His body was exhumed in 1784 and a 30 inch thigh bone suggested a height of around eight feet. The church has some fine Eyre brasses.

Charlotte Bronte must have been intrigued by the history of the Eyre family when she stayed in Hathersage, for she used much of the material in her novel, Jayne Eyre. North Lees was her model for Thornfield.

Hathersage is a good base from which to explore the gritstone edges, Carl Wark and Padley Gorge.

4.11 Padley Hall

Padley Hall was a 14th century manor house built by the Eyres. In 1588, the year of the Armada, two Catholic priests (Nicholas Garlick and Robert Ludham) were found hiding at Padley Hall. The Crown saw Catholic priests as subversives, who were likely to support an invasion, and Garlick and Ludham were hung, drawn and quartered. The owner of the Hall, John Fitzherbert of Norbury (see 5.8 River Dove walk) was imprisoned for harbouring the priests and died in the Tower of London.

Subsequently, the Hall fell into disrepair. The chapel, which is the only building standing, was used first as a cowshed and then by the navvies building the Totley tunnel for the Manchester-Sheffield railway line. It was reopened as a chapel in 1933.

4.12 Rowsley

Rowsley is a small village almost wholly owned by the Duke of Rutland. The Peacock Hotel is Rowsley's best-known building. Formerly Rowsley Hall, it was built for Lady Manners in 1652. (The Manners family crest, a stone peacock, stands above the door).

Rowsley was previously an important railway station, with milk being despatched daily to London. The railway depot was closed in 1960, but Paxton's station of 1849 still survives on an industrial estate. The Station Hotel was renamed the Claret and Grouse.

Cauldwell's Mill, standing on the River Wye near its confluence with the Derwent, operated from 1874 to 1974 as a cornmill, fulling mill and sawmill, using turbines rather than waterwheels. It has now been fully restored and is a craft centre.

4.13 Stanton Moor and the Nine Ladies Circle

Over seventy barrows and cairns on Stanton Moor associated with the Bronze Age were excavated by the father and son team of J C and J P Heathcote. Much of the material they found is displayed in the Sheffield Museum.

The Nine Ladies Circle was originally a burial barrow. Removal of the surrounding soil now gives it the appearance of a henge.

The tower on Stanton Moor Edge was erected in honour of Earl Grey's part in the 1832 Reform Act. The site was carefully chosen to ensure that it would be seen by both the Dukes of Rutland and of Devonshire.

4.14 Winster

This is a delightful village with sixty listed buildings, the most prominent being the Market House. Built in 1700, the Market House now belongs to the National Trust.

The former prosperity of Winster was based on lead, and the hills around the village are pockmarked with lead spoil heaps.

Winster was also an important market town, and its success may be judged by the number of its pubs. In the 18th century, when the population of Winster was about 200, the pubs numbered 22! One Public House which survived Winster's subsequent decline in prosperity is the Miners Standard Inn. Sited above the village, on the road to Bonsall, the Inn has an interesting collection of mining memorabilia.

There have been several earthquakes at Winster. The last, in 1952, was serious enough to result in structural damage. The cause is thought to be the local geology rather than mining subsidence.

4.15 Wirksworth

Situated at the head of the Ecclesbourne valley, Wirksworth was an important lead mining centre, possibly as early as Roman times. Local tradition has it that nearby Middleton was a Roman slave camp for the mines.

Before the Norman Conquest, the Wirksworth lead mining rights belonged to the Mercian royal abbey at Repton. One of the most important Anglo-Saxon sculptures in the country, the Wirksworth Stone, dates from the time when the Peak District was part of the Mercian Kingdom.

The focal point of the town is St Mary's Church. Although the fabric is mainly 13th century, there are Norman elements in the transepts. In addition to the Wirksworth Stone, there are some fine alabasters of the Gell family and a brass of Thomas Blackwell.

The town is mainly 17th and 18th century and imaginative restoration work is bringing it back to its former glory. The life of the town is displayed in the Heritage Centre.

Quarrying has been the other important economic activity in Wirksworth. The high quality of the Hopton Wood limestone Marble led to it being used in many important buildings including Westminster Abbey and York Minister. The National Stone Centre just to the north of Wirksworth on the High Peak Trail tells the story of stone.

Walk 5: River Dove

Distances:

Total: 27 miles

Section 1: Axe Edge to Hartington: 9.6 miles

Section 2: Hartington to Thorpe Cloud: 7.7 miles

Section 3: Thorpe Cloud to Rocester: 9.7 miles

Ordnance Survey map: Outdoor Leisure 24, The White Peak

The Dove (from the Anglo-Saxon *Duba* meaning dark) is perhaps the best-known of the Peak District rivers. The valley offers three distinctly different types of scenery, a reflection of the different types of rocks through which the river runs

¤ from the source on the bleak Axe Edge to Hartington, the river runs through shale which produces rounded hillsides. Although the river first encounters limestone reef knolls near Hollinsclough it is initially unable to penetrate this harder rock and runs along the interface between the limestone and the shale

¤ near Hartington the river finally breaches the line of the reef knolls. For the next dozen miles the river runs through the best-known part of the valley – the Dove of Izaac Walton's "The Compleat Angler" and, in a succession of limestone dales (Beresford Dale, Wolfscote Dale, Milldale, Hall Dale and Dovedale), are found the limestone cliffs, pinnacles and caves so popular with the Victorians

¤ at Thorpe, the Dove is joined by the Manifold and flows out of the limestone into sandstone. This more rounded countryside is less spectacular and therefore less popular than the limestone dales but is, nevertheless, delightful walking country.

The valley is predominantly agricultural, and the flora is largely determined by the underlying geology:

¤ poor grassland in the shales of the upper reaches

¤ good grassland on the limestone hills. (Many sheep granges of medieval monasteries were sited on these limestone hills)

¤ typical limestone flowers in the dales between Hartington and Thorpe (cowslips, early purple orchids, rock roses, violets, saxifrage and wild thyme)

¤ good agricultural land in the alluvial valley below Thorpe.

The paths at the head of the valley, many of which are former packhorse routes, are little used and not well-signposted. If you intend to walk this part of the valley, it is recommended that you augment the maps in this book with the Outdoor Leisure Ordnance Survey map.

The Dove valley at Pilsbury

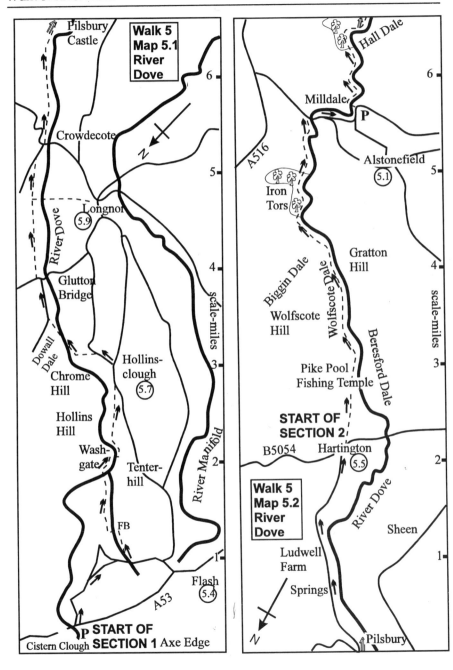

Walk 5 Map 5.1 River Dove

Pilsbury Castle

Crowdecote

Longnor (5.9)

River Dove

Glutton Bridge

Dowall Dale

Chrome Hill

Hollins Hill

Hollins-clough (5.7)

Wash-gate

Tenter-hill

FB

River Manifold

scale-miles

6

5

4

3

2

1

Flash (5.4)

A53

P **START OF**

Cistern Clough **SECTION 1** Axe Edge

Walk 5 Map 5.2 River Dove

Hall Dale

Milldale P

Alstonefield (5.1)

A516

Iron Tors

Biggin Dale

Wolfscote Dale

Gratton Hill

Wolfscote Hill

Beresford Dale

Pike Pool Fishing Temple

START OF SECTION 2

B5054 Hartington (5.5)

River Dove

Sheen

Ludwell Farm

Springs

Pilsbury

scale-miles

6

5

4

3

2

1

N

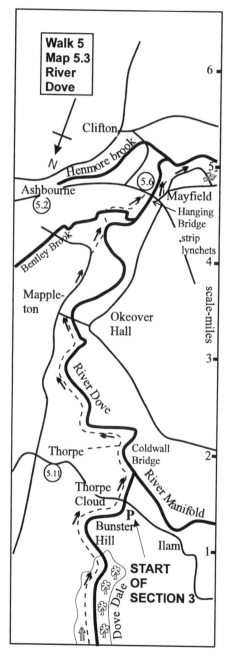

Walk 5
Map 5.3
River
Dove

N

Clifton

Henmore brook

Ashbourne
5.2

Bentley Brook

5.6

Mayfield
Hanging
Bridge
strip
lynchets

Mapple-
ton

Okeover
Hall

scale-miles

River Dove

Thorpe
5.11

Coldwall
Bridge

River Manifold

Thorpe
Cloud

P

Bunster
Hill

Ilam

START
OF
SECTION 3

Dove Dale

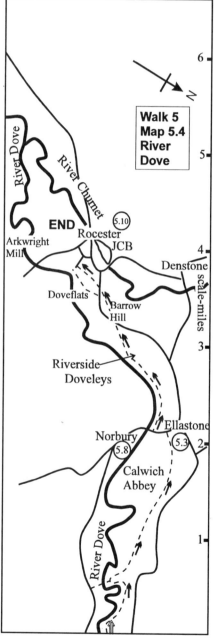

Walk 5
Map 5.4
River
Dove

N

River Dove

River Churnet

Arkwright
Mill

END Rocester
5.10
JCB

Denstone

Doveflats

Barrow
Hill

scale-miles

Riverside
Doveleys

Norbury
5.8

Ellastone
5.3

Calwich
Abbey

River Dove

The Walk

Section 1: Axe Edge to Hartington

Distance: 9.6 miles

Starting point: SK035698

Maps: 5.1 and 5.2

The Dove rises on Axe Edge in a field below the A53. A convenient place to start the walk is from the car park about a mile from the source, where a tributary of the Dove runs under the A53 at Cistern's Clough.

From this car park, cross the A53 and take the minor road which descends the hill. When the road divides, take the right fork. At the stream, (the nascent Dove), cross the bridge and take the footpath which climbs the hill to the left.

Follow the uphill edge of the fence at the top of the first field above the river. When the path meets another coming down from a farmhouse on the right, take the path to the left which goes down a steep gully to a footbridge. Cross the bridge, and take the path which climbs diagonally uphill towards a farmhouse. Before actually reaching the farmhouse, the path descends towards the river. Do not take the path across the river, but keep to the east bank to meet the junction of the Dove with its tributary coming down from Cistern's Clough.

A short distance downstream, the path comes to the packhorse bridge at Washgate which must be one of the most attractive to be seen in the Peak District.

From Washgate, take the path along the west side of the river towards Hollinsclough about a mile away. This path rises, traverses the hillside and then descends to the river with some excellent views of the limestone reef knolls on the other side of the river – Hollins Hill, Chrome Hill, Parkhouse Hill and Hitter Hill. Just before reach-

Washgate

ing Hollinsclough there is another packhorse bridge over the Dove, but this is not nearly as attractive as the one at Washgate.

On entering Hollinsclough, there is a Victorian post box set in the wall on the right. Bear left at the Methodist church in the centre of the village to head towards the river.

Upstream of Hollinsclough the Dove had been confined to the narrow channel it had cut itself. Now the flat valley bottom is almost a mile across.

About a quarter of a mile down the road from Hollinsclough, take the path to the left over a cattlegrid and past a barn. Follow this to a footbridge and cross the river. About fifty yards after the river there is a cutting at the side of the track which exposes the underlying rock. Notice that, in spite of the fact that there are limestone reef knolls in front, the river is still running in shale.

To your left is Dowel Dale. When excavated, the cave at the top of this dale yielded ten neolithic bodies.

The path ahead joins the byroad to Glutton Bridge where you turn left and then almost immediately right into the minor road towards Crowdecote. About half way to Crowdecote you will cross a path to the right going down to Beggar's Bridge and then to Longnor. Here the Dove and Manifold rivers are only a mile apart. If you wish to cross from one valley to the other, this is a convenient place to do so.

The name of the pub at Crowdecote, The Packhorse Inn, is a reflection of the fact that this was formerly a river crossing point for several packhorse routes. (The original inn was actually next door to the present pub).

From Crowdecote, keep to the eastern bank of the river and, in just over a mile, the Norman motte and bailey of Pilsbury Castle is reached. Some of the exposed rock surfaces at the side of the path in the Pilsbury area have wild thyme growing on them. Even if not in flower, thyme is easily recognised by the pungent aroma produced when rubbed between the fingers.

From Pilsbury, a single track road leads to Hartington two miles away. In the region of Ludwell Farm there are a number of springs flowing out of the limestone. Some flow overground into the river, and others bubble directly into the riverbed. Notice how the water coming out of the limestone is considerably clearer than that of the main body of the river which originated in the shales.

As you have proceeded down the valley from Hollinsclough, there have been reef knolls to your left. Ahead they are now across the valley and, after Hartington, the river will finally pass out of the shales into the limestone.

Hartington is an attractive village which is worth exploring. In addition to the village square, the church and the 17th century Hartington Hall which is now a Youth Hostel are worthy of note.

Section 2: Hartington to Thorpe Cloud

Distance: 7.7 miles

Starting point: SK130604

Maps: 5.2 and 5.3

The path out of Hartington is just to the west of the centre of the village, between the pottery and the public conveniences, and crosses open countryside towards the gap between Wolfscote Hill and Gratton Hill. As you approach the woodlands you will see a tower on the hillside, all that remains of Charles Cotton's Beresford Hall. Below, close to the river and almost hidden by trees, is the famous fishing temple used by Cotton and his friend Izaac Walton.

The first pool on entering the wood is the Pike Pool, referred to in *The Compleat Angler*. It is so called, not because of some medieval monster fish, but because Walton saw in the limestone pillar a resemblance to a pike.

After Beresford Dale you come to the more open Wolfscote Dale with its rock roses, violets, saxifrage and wild thyme.

At Iron Tors there are the remains of a ram pump, to the left of the path, which supplied water to the farm above. These ingenious devices required no external power, using only the kinetic energy of the water to pump a small amount of water to a higher level.

Two former mills are passed – at Lode Mill and at Milldale. The bridge at Milldale is the Viator's packhorse bridge of the Compleat

Angler. About a mile above Milldale is the very attractive village of Alstonefield which may be reached by footpath.

When Hall Dale is reached, look out for early purple orchids and cowslips if it is late spring or early summer. In the ash woods of Dovedale itself are the numerous limestone caves, cliffs and pinnacles so beloved by the Victorians who named them.

The river leaves Dovedale between Thorpe Cloud and Bunster Hill. It is well worth the steep climb up Thorpe Cloud for the extensive views down the Dove. On a clear day it is possible to see right down to the river Trent with its power stations, and to the hills on the other side of the Trent valley.

If you are finishing your walk at Thorpe Cloud, cross to the west side of the river to get to the car park. Otherwise, keep to the east bank.

The lower valley from Thorpe Cloud

Section 3: Thorpe Cloud to Rocester

Distance: 9.7 miles

Starting point: SK146509

Maps: 5.3 and 5.4

If there are crowds in Dovedale, these should evaporate after Thorpe Cloud for, despite the attractiveness of the countryside, few people walk downstream here.

Shortly, the Dove is joined by the Manifold and the river flow becomes much more substantial. The Manifold, draining a much larger catchment area than the Dove, is the larger of the two rivers, but the combined river keeps the name of the Dove since it is the county boundary.

About a mile from Thorpe Cloud the path comes to Coldwall Bridge, a relic of the turnpike era. When the turnpike ceased to operate, this section of the road became redundant, leaving the unusual sight of a substantial bridge going nowhere. If you wish to visit Thorpe, take the path up from the bridge.

From Coldwall Bridge, the path ahead follows the river bank to the village of Mapleton. At Mapleton follow the minor road towards Ashbourne for three quarters of a mile.

As the road begins to swing towards the east, take the path to the right across the fields. This skirts the river and then crosses the Bentley Brook before coming out onto the Ashbourne to Leek Road near the Hanging Bridge at Mayfield.

If you look up on the western hillside as you approach Mayfield, you will see the strip lynchets which are so characteristic of medieval agriculture.

Cross the Hanging Bridge and, taking the road to the left, look back under the bridge. You can now see why this ordinary modern bridge is a listed monument. Under the modern structure is a beautiful medieval bridge. It was over this bridge that Bonnie Prince Charlie marched in 1745 on his way to Derby, and it was over the same bridge that he retreated two days later.

About a hundred yards after the bridge, take the path to the left which follows the riverbank. The path comes out in Church May-

Coldwall Bridge

field where you should follow the road past the church until you reach a path across the fields towards the river.

Follow the path along the riverbank until a footbridge is reached crossing the Dove (Toadhole Bridge). Do not cross the river, but take the path to the west towards the hillside.

Climb the hill and follow the contour past some farm buildings towards the site of the former Calwich Abbey. Never apparently a successful Abbey, Calwich had only six monks at the Dissolution of the Monasteries.

Near the Abbey site, notice the copper-domed "fishing temple" down by the river. The composer Handel was a frequent visitor to Calwich and there is a story that it was here that he is said to have composed his Water Music.

The path then descends from Calwich to Ellastone. At Ellastone, the path leads dowstream from the bridge, on the west side of the river. Here, the river is a pleasant sequence of pools and short rapids.

A large Victorian mansion with grounds running down to the river is reached at Riverside Doveleys. In autumn the cherry laurel at the river's edge is very attractive with its red berries (a plant favoured by the Victorians and therefore probably over a century old).

The path goes into the woods for a short distance and then climbs diagonally across a number of fields to join the road above just below a farmhouse. Looking back as you climb there are good views over the Weaver Hills to the north of Ellastone.

At the road, there is a choice to be made between barbed wire and a short distance along a busy road. The first and proper choice is to take the path over the stile at the other side of the road and to descend the fields. On the 1:25,000 map this path crosses the road to Barrowhill and then cuts diagonally across the small rectangular field to emerge onto the road. The difficulty is that the stile at the bottom of the field has barbed wire across it, and has been allowed to become overgrown with brambles. The path over the road to Rocester is a few yards downhill and, although well-concealed in the hedge, is passable.

If you don't like barbed wire and bramble hopping, the alternative choice is to follow the busy road for about a third of a mile until the farm of Doveflats is reached (the sign of a horse at the roadside).

Although the footpath is not marked, there is a right of way down the farm track and then over the fields to Rocester below.

Whichever route is chosen down to Rocester, the view of the town is dominated by two industrial enterprises of very different periods:

¤ Arkwright's textile mill on the River Dove

¤ JCB, the modern earth moving company on the Churnet.

Places of interest in the Dove valley

5.1 Alstonefield

Alstonefield, a quiet village just above Milldale, has some fine old buildings including the Hall of 1587 and a 12th century church. Many stone fragments in the church suggest the foundation is much older, going back to Saxon times. Charles Cotton, Izaac Walton's fishing companion, worshipped at the church and his family pew is a feature of interest. Also of note is a magnificent carved pulpit. Evidently the 16th century craftsmen were efficiency experts for they shortened the text to "I will give thee a crown etc". The George, a public house on the green, is popular with walkers.

5.2 Ashbourne

Esseburne of the Domesday Book is an attractive town on the Henmore, a tributary of the Dove. It has many excellent Georgian buildings and one of the finest churches in the Peak District.

A touch of local colour is a two day annual football match with few rules which is played along the Henmore Brook on Shrove Tuesday and Ash Wednesday. One of the goal posts is in the field adjacent to the Henmore Brook just below the village of Clifton.

5.3 Ellastone

From the architecture of some of its buildings, Ellastone was obviously at one time a place of some standing (one wonders how much of the stonework in the buildings hereabouts came courtesy of the dissolved Monastery of Calwich).

Until the 19th century, North Staffordshire was important for its ironstone and Ellastone is recorded in 1483 as having an iron works. In the 18th century some of the copper from the Duke of Devonshire's Ecton Mine was smelted here.

George Eliot, the author, was a resident of Ellastone.

To the north are the Weaver Hills with their neolithic burial tumuli.

5.4 Flash

Flash, a place where several packhorse routes met, is the highest village in England.

Its name entered the English language when villagers were discovered counterfeiting in 1812. Flash was well-placed for counterfeiting, being near the border between the three counties of Staffordshire, Derbyshire and Cheshire. At the time, the police had no authority outside their own county and miscreants could easily avoid capture by crossing to another county.

A legal local industry was button making, the last button maker only dying in 1987.

5.5 Hartington

Hartington suffered badly under the Norman Conquest, but had reestablished itself by 1203 when it was granted the first charter in the Peak District to hold a market.

The village, which is a popular tourist centre and can be crowded, has a most attractive Square with some fine buildings and a duck pond. The three public houses are former Coaching Inns.

Hartington Hall, built in 1611 for the Bateman family, is one of many excellent small manor houses throughout the Peak District built during the 17th century. It is now a Youth Hostel.

Cheese has been manufactured in Hartington since 1870. Unlike other Peak District cheese factories which have come and gone, the Hartington factory still thrives, making Stilton. Cheese may be bought in "Ye Olde Cheese Shoppe" in the village Square.

5.6 Hanging Bridge, Mayfield

The Roman Road from Chesterfield to Rocester is thought to have crossed the Dove in the vicinity of the Hanging Bridge. The Roman Road later became known as Hereward Way and a document of 1330 mentions "Herwardstrete" passing close by.

Bonnie Prince Charlie crossed the bridge with his army twice in 1745 on his unsuccessful campaign to seize the crown.

The medieval bridge may be seen nestling below the structure of the modern road bridge.

5.7 Hollinsclough

Hollinsclough was formerly a silk weaving centre. Two packhorse routes cross the Dove just to the north of the village and it is perhaps of no surprise that a local minister, John Lomas (1747-1823), was a strong advocate for packhorse men, making representations to the Prime Minister on their behalf. John Lomas built the Methodist Chapel in 1801, and his initials are to be seen over the door.

5.8 Norbury

Just over the Dove from Ellastone is Norbury, the home for many centuries of the Fitzherbert family who came to Britain with William the Conqueror.

Next to the remains of the 13th century manor is one of Derbyshire's finest churches. Of particular note are the 14th century chancel and the alabaster tomb of Sir Nicholas Fitzherbert with his wife and 17 children.

In the 16th century Sir John Fitzherbert of Norbury became the owner of Padley Hall on the river Derwent after his marriage to a daughter of the Eyre family. In common with many other of the most important families in the Peak District, Sir John paid the price of being of the wrong religious persuasion. When Catholic priests were found hiding in Padley Hall, he was arrested and imprisoned in the Tower of London where he died. His status as a knight saved him from the more dramatic fate of the two priests who were hung, drawn and quartered.

5.9 Longnor (see Manifold)

5.10 Rocester

Rocester is a small town sandwiched between the rivers Dove and Churnet. A Roman fort was sited at Rocester and a number of Roman artefacts were discovered when the foundations of the cotton mill were dug. Arkwright established a mill on the Dove in 1781-2 and today Rocester is the home of the earth moving company, JCB.

Contemporary Rocester is a mixture of attractive cottages and a less happy legacy of 1960s architecture.

5.11 Thorpe

Thorpe was originally a Danish settlement, probably established during the Viking raids around AD875. Its church has an exquisite Norman tower thought to date from around 1100.

Although now a quiet backwater, Thorpe was an important transport centre in the 18th century being on two turnpike roads, both having relatively short lives. The section of the Ashbourne to Buxton turnpike was bypassed in 1777 when a new road was built through Fenny Bentley. Later, the turnpike heading westwards also became redundant. Unlike many other such roads which then become minor roads serving local traffic, the road over Coldwall bridge fell into disuse. This is why today there is the unusual sight of Coldwall Bridge over the Dove leading nowhere. The pub, the Dog and Partridge, was originally a Coaching Inn.

Behind the village is Thorpe Cloud which at 942 feet affords magnificent views over the bottom of the Dove and Manifold valleys and as far south as the Trent. The word Cloud is thought to have no connection with the sky, but rather to be derived from Clud, an Old English word meaning rock or hill.

Walk 6: River Etherow

Distances

Total: 19.7 miles

Section 1: Crowden Car Park to Hadfield: 5.6 miles

Section 2: Hadfield to Compstall: 6.6 miles

Reservoir circular walk: 7.5 miles

Ordnance Survey map: Outdoor Leisure 1, The Dark Peak. (This covers Section 1 and the circular walk. Section 2 is straightforward and requires only the map in this book).

Above the Etherow valley

The Etherow valley is under-rated as a walking area compared with many other parts of the Peak District, but you should not be put off by the electricity pylons and the busy main road in the valley bottom. The best walks are high on the hillsides well away from these modern intrusions.

Although peat covers large areas of the Peak District, the flat hilltops on which it sits often have restricted views and make the walking rather uninteresting. The Etherow valley is an exception, providing some excellent walks along the interface between the peat moorland and the gritstone crags and boulder strewn slopes below. Here is an area which combines a rugged wilderness with fine views over the valley below and the distant hills.

The landscapes of the upper and lower sections of the Etherow valley are quite different in character because of the different types of underlying rock:

¤ hard gritstone in the upper valley leads to a U-shaped valley below high peat moorlands

¤ softer shales and coal measures in the lower valley (below the reservoirs) give lower hilltops and a valley which is broader and more pastoral.

Flints which are washing out of a site on the bank of the Torside reservoir show that the valley was settled in prehistoric times. The next firm evidence of settlement is in the Roman times, the camp at Melandra being one of a chain of forts built in the AD70s to subjugate the Brigantes.

It is thought that the Normans came down Longdendale during the "harrying of the north" and, at the time of the Domesday Survey, the dozen "vills" in Longdendale were all recorded as "waste".

The Etherow was next established as the northern boundary of the King's Peak Forest, thus ensuring that it would remain undeveloped for several centuries.

The availability of water power and locally mined coal led to early industrialisation of the valley with a large number of mills established along the length of the river. Manchester's need for water in the early 19th century however, was even more pressing and the building of five reservoirs led to the de-industialisation of the upper valley.

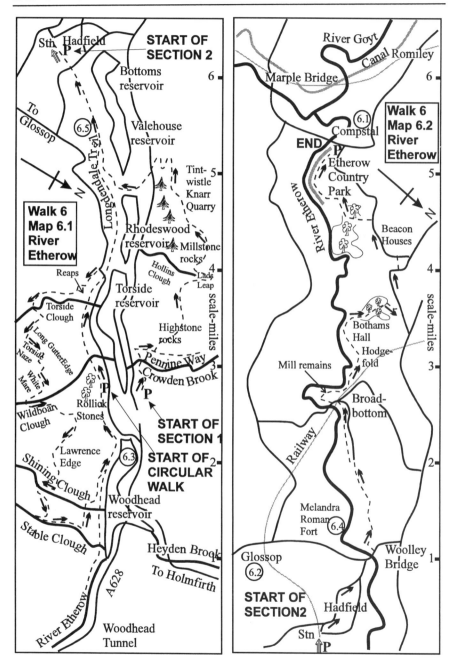

The Walk

Section 1: Crowden Car Park to Hadfield

Distance: 5.6 miles

Starting point: SK073994

Map: 6.1

From the car park at Crowden on the north side of the Torside Reservoir, take the path which leads past the camping site and over the Crowden Brook. Climb the hill, go through a gate and, just before a small wood, turn right along the Pennine Way. Follow this path until you reach a stile and cross. You are now on Access Land and do not need to keep to the paths.

Leave the Pennine Way by taking the path to the left which climbs upwards some 800 feet to the moorland above. The last part of the climb is up a gentle slope between banks of peat.

When you reach the top, you are on a flat plateau at an elevation of about 1500 feet. Follow the line of the wall to the edge of the slope to see the views up and down the valley. In the distance you should be able to see the hills on the western edge of the Peak District. Notice that these hills are much more "peaky" than the flat gritstone peaks. The reason for this difference is that, during a period of earth movement some 300 million years ago, the western edge of the Peak District was subject to much more buckling than was the central region.

Almost directly south on the horizon, the steep slope of Kinder Scout should be visible as it descends to Ashop Head. (At the foot of that slope is the Snake Pass, followed on the Ashop valley walk).

Follow the hillside edge to Lad's Leap. Here Hollins Clough has cut back into the gritstone hillside forcing you away from the reservoir. Cross Lad's Leap and follow the path along Millstone Rocks before descending to the Tintwistle Knarr Quarry. There is a path both above and below the quarry. Take the lower route across the quarry face.

Follow the path down from the quarry. When the path follows an S curve, ignore two paths to the left but take the third which goes down to the main road. Cross the road taking the path down to and over the Rhodeswood Reservoir dam. Here, follow the minor road on the other side of the reservoir to the point where you may join the Longdendale Trail.

Follow the Trail for about a mile and a half past Valehouse and Bottoms Reservoirs to reach the end of the Trail near Hadfield station.

There is a car park at the end of the Longdendale Trail just before Hadfield Station.

Section 2: Hadfield to Compstall

Distance: 6.6 miles

Starting point: SK 024961 (car Park near Hadfield Station)

Map: 6.2

If you are proceeding further down the valley you will need to walk about a mile through the built up area to Woolley Bridge. Just after the railway station there is a bridge. Turn right at the bridge and follow the road through Hadfield to Woolley Bridge.

You will reach the river at Woolley Bridge just to the east of the bridge. Cross the bridge, and follow the busy main road for about 100 yards before reaching a turn to the left to Woolley Farm.

From here to Compstall you will be following a path known as the Valley Way which is reasonably well-signposted with yellow markers on a red background.

After the farm, you cross a wide valley bottom. Notice on the other side of the river, perched on high ground just above the river, the site of the Roman Fort of Melandra.

When the hillside is reached, climb upwards to Pear Tree Farm. Just after the farm, the path divides. Take the top path and then bear left around some farm buildings onto a track which takes you towards Broadbottom.

At Broadbottom the river meets a band of hard gritstone and curves left through a ravine it has carved 100 feet below. The railway takes advantage of the narrowest crossing of the ravine to span the river.

Follow the road under the railway bridge and for a further 200 yards downhill before turning right down to the Lymefield Information Centre (open Saturday and Sunday). Proceed downhill and turn right in front of Lymefield Terrace towards the remains of Broad Mill. Built by William and George Sidebottom, this was a cotton spinning and weaving mill which operated between 1802 and 1920. The Valley Way goes through the restored foundations and there are a number of display boards.

A little further along the river, you will come to another interesting restoration. Here there are a large number of vats made out of gritstone flags at what was once a dye works.

Leaving Broadbottom you will pass an attractive cottage, Hodgefold, dated 1676. Turn left here and follow the path to the river.

When Botham Hall is reached, the path bears right and you follow it uphill before taking the path to the left into the woods. At the top of the woods, skirt the first field and then cross the second field diagonally to reach a minor road next to a farm.

Turn left onto this road. In just under half a mile, the road bears right and climbs steeply with serrations in the concrete surface to increase the traction. Take the path to the left into the fields. Above you are two radio beacons.

When the path through the field rejoins the minor road bear left. The elevation here is about 700 feet and there are extensive views not only up and down the valley but of –

¤ the hills on the eastern edge of the Peak District

¤ Alderley Edge sticking out into the Cheshire plain

¤ on the horizon, the Welsh hills and Liverpool Cathedral

When a path is reached which goes to the left towards a wooded ravine, it will take you to the Etherow Country Park. At the valley bottom a weir supplies a half mile canal which runs down to Compstall Mill. This canal provided both water for the mill and a method of transporting coal from the colliery on the other side of the river. A coal barge may be seen on the bank at the top of the canal.

Follow the path at the side of the canal. You will notice that the rock which outcrops at the side of the path is not the gritstone seen higher up the valley but rather a friable shale. This is characteristic of rock of the Lower Coal Measure. (The coal seam mined in this area was known as Yard Coal because it was a yard thick).

At the end of the canal you will come to the car park.

Reservoir Circular Walk

Distance: 7.5 miles

Starting point: SK068983

Map: 6.1

The walk starts at the National Park Information Centre on the south side of the Torside Reservoir. Take the path from the car park up to join the Longdendale Trail. Follow the Trail west for just under a mile and turn left onto the Pennine Way.

Leave the Pennine Way just after it has made a detour round a farmhouse named Reaps, by taking a track which traverses the hillside to the brook in Torside Clough.

Just before the track reaches the brook, a path bears left over the brook. If the brook is in flood, you may need to cross a little higher up, scrambling back over the boulders to the first crossing point.

Look up from the crossing to see a fence high up on Torside Naze. It is this fence line which you will be climbing to join. You are now on Access Land where there are no formal paths and you need to make your way upwards using rudimentary tracks and sometimes sheep tracks. The skill is in choosing a line upwards which avoids the boggy areas.

A zigzag path goes upwards under long Gutter Edge and then appears to peter out. In passing between Long Gutter Edge and

Torside Naze, keep close to the base of Torside Naze to avoid the large flat boggy expanse at the back of Long Gutter Edge.

Continue to climb upwards until you meet the fence and cross the stile. From here, there are good views of the Pennine Way on both sides of the valley.

Follow the fence line to the east but, before meeting a fence climbing up the hillside, climb upwards over the gritstone boulders. (If you leave it too late before climbing you will end up on a stretch of boggy peat).

At the hilltop there should be a stile to your left which you cross. Look out here for mountain hares on the boulder strewn slopes beneath you. During the winter months the hares have white coats, the theory being that this camouflages them against the snow. In practice, when there is no snow on the ground, they are extremely conspicuous.

For the next two miles follow the interface between the peat and the gritstone slopes. This is marvellous rugged country with splendid views over the valley and the hills to the north.

After passing White Mare, you will come to Wildboar Clough which is a deep clough formed in the hillside by a small brook. Here you will need to track someway up the clough before being able to descend to the brook to cross.

After Wildboar Clough, cross the top of Rollick Stones, which is a large gritstone landslip. Notice at the bottom of Rollick Stones an oakwood which is typical of relict oakwoods on inaccessible hillsides throughout the Peak District (inaccessible both to man and grazing animals).

Passing Lawrence Edge you will come to Shining Clough, which again may only be crossed by following the clough some way away from the reservoirs.

The next clough reached is Stable Clough and, when you descend to the clough bottom, you will pick up a shooters track which you follow down towards the reservoirs.

The stretch of the track through the grounds of The Lodge is private, and the path follows a detour to the left, along the fence around this estate (boggy in places).

At a small pond, the path bears right and goes down to the track coming out of The Lodge. Follow this to join the Longdendale Trail near the foot of the Woodhead reservoir.

On the way back to the car park you will pass the old Crowden railway cottages and the old Torside Paper Mill which is now a dwelling (at the bottom of Fair Vage Gutter).

Places of interest in the Etherow valley

6.1 Compstall

Medieval monastic records show that coal was mined at Compstall in the Middle Ages when the mines belonged to Basingwerk Abbey in Clwyd.

In the early 1800s, George and Thomas Andrew established a textile business at Compstall using a half mile canal feeder from the Etherow to power the mill waterwheels. Steam power was introduced in 1833 using locally mined coal and gas lighting was introduced to the mill in 1834. Today the area has become part of the Etherow Country Park.

6.2 Glossop

Although a market charter was granted to Glossop in 1290, the town we see today was largely built in the 17th and 19th centuries. There are some fine 17th century houses in Old Glossop and the Duke of Norfolk laid out a "planned" textile town in the 19th century at the intersection of three turnpikes.

On the western edge of the town stands the Roman fort of Melandra and a Roman road joins Melandra and Navio on the River Noe. It was largely along this Roman road that Dr John Talbot, Vicar of Glossop (1494-1550) and illegitimate son of the Earl of Shrewsbury, travelled to his father's castle at Sheffield. The road thereafter became known as Doctor's Gate.

6.3 The Longdendale Reservoirs

In the early 19th century the link between pollution and disease was established which created an enormous demand from the cities for the supply of clean water. The problem was compounded by the high population growth in the previous century. It was fortunate for Manchester that, sitting on its doorstep, was the Longdendale Valley (valley of the upper Etherow) with its catchment area of 26 square miles and an average rainfall of 52 inches.

In 1845, the Water Engineer John Bateman started work on the first of five reservoirs which were to take him 29 years to complete. Water for public supply is taken mainly from Rhodeswood via a tunnel to the Arnfield Treatment Works. The bottom two reservoirs provide compensation water for the River Etherow.

The total storage capacity of the reservoirs is some 4000 million gallons with 30 million gallons a day being supplied to Manchester and 10 million gallons a day to the River Etherow.

The building of the reservoirs led to the inundation of several hamlets (Torside, Vale House and Bottoms) and several works (Torside Paper Mill, Crowden Bleach Works, Vale House and Bottoms Lodge Cotton Mills). A house at the foot of Fair Vage Clough (SK079990) was originally a paper mill.

The reservoirs at dusk

6.4 Melandra

Within five years of the invasion of Britain in AD43, the Romans had extended their new province to the Trent. There was no initial need for them to settle Brigantia since there was a friendly alliance between the Romans and the Queen of the Brigantes.

In AD 69 however, following Civil War in Brigantia, an anti-Roman faction took power forcing the Romans to act.

Strategically sited overlooking the River Etherow, Melandra was one of a chain of forts established by the Romans to subjugate Brigantia. The three acre site was first occupied in the AD70s and was abandoned in the AD140s when troops were withdrawn to strengthen the Roman presence in Scotland.

In hostile territory, Roman forts were normally sited within a day's march of each other (10-12 miles). It is surmised that a fort is still to be found further up Longdendale. (Recent survey work has uncovered what looks like a fortlet on the 900 ft contour near Highstones Rocks).

Legend has it that Roman soldiers used the British Iron Age site at Torside Castle (just off the Pennine Way at SK 077966) as a burial site and that the ghosts of Roman soldiers are to be seen roaming the bleak moors.

6.5 The Woodhead Railway Line

The line operated for 136 years from its opening in 1845. It was closed to passenger services in 1970 and freight in 1981. Today the railway terminates at Hadfield.

Three 3 mile tunnels were built at Woodhead opening in 1845, 1849 and 1954 (the last being electrified). The first two tunnels were built at the very high cost of 32 killed and 500 seriously injured.

On closure of the line, one of the tunnels was converted to take the 400kV electricity link to avoid disfiguring the skyline with pylons.

The 6.8 miles of the former track between the Woodhead Tunnel and Hadfield station have been converted into the Longdendale Trail, a footpath and bridleway.

Walk 7: River Goyt

Distances:

Total: 18 miles

Section 1: Derbyshire Bridge to Whaley Bridge: 8.4 miles

Section 2: Whaley Bridge to Compstall: 9.6 miles

Ordnance Survey Maps: Outdoor Leisure 1, The Dark Peak; Outdoor Leisure 24, The White Peak. (These maps cover the valley from the source down to New Mills only. The walk downstream from New Mills to Compstall is straightforward, requiring only the maps in this book.)

It is possible to walk the entire length of this popular valley from the source of the river to its confluence with the Etherow at Compstall. The walk includes sections along riverbank, reservoir, canal and redundant railway line, together with excursions to higher ground which give views over the valley below.

The rocks of the Goyt valley are shale, gritstone and coal measures. Up to Whaley Bridge, there are significant glacial deposits in the valley bottom left over from the last Ice Age. The largest of these is a moraine at New Mills which blocked the former channel of the Goyt. Diverted to the east, the river cut the spectacular gorge known as the Torrs.

With its coal and water resources, the Goyt valley developed rapidly in the 19th century into one of the world's major textile producing centres. Today only one major mill remain, at Strines.

The valley contains a high concentration of transportation routes. Early routes crossed the top of the valley (a Roman Road and two saltways) and the Industrial Revolution brought canal, railway and roads along the bottom of the valley. Because of the difficult terrain, these communication routes required spectacular and expensive engineering solutions.

Although the Goyt has its share of conifer plantations around the reservoirs, it also has a significant number of deciduous trees. These are particularly attractive in the autumn. The grounds of the former Errwood Hall are notable for their rhododendrons and azaleas.

Thoughout its length, the valley is well-supplied with car parks. A traffic flow system is operated above Errwood Reservoir. During the week, traffic is only allowed up the valley, and at the weekend the road is reserved for pedestrians.

Goytsclough

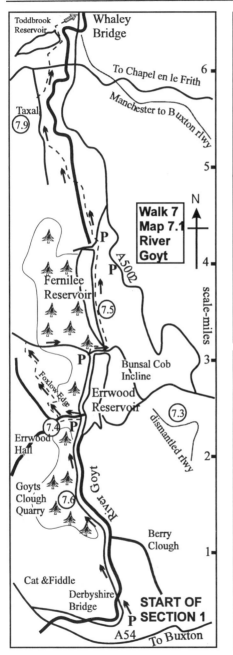

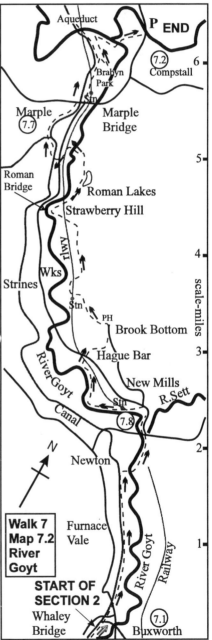

The Walk

Section 1: Derbyshire Bridge to Whaley Bridge
Distance: 5.6 miles
Starting point: SK 018716
Map: 7.1

From the car park just off the A54, take the road which follows the river downstream. In about a quarter of a mile, Derbyshire Bridge is reached, so called because the Goyt was at one time on the Cheshire/Derbyshire boundary (this boundary is now a mile to the west).

For the first mile from the car park the landscape is treeless, the ground cover being heather and bracken. The underlying rocks are of friable shale and low quality coal was once mined in this area. The first trees are met at the Goytsclough Quarry. There is a conifer plantation on the hillside to the left and deciduous trees in the valley below. The quarry produced good quality paving stones from well-bedded gritstone. Below the quarry a 300 year old packhorse bridge crosses the river.

The mile from the quarry to the Errwood Reservoir is a most attractive walk through mixed woodlands with the river running below. When the car park near the head of the reservoir is reached, follow the path to the left to the site of Errwood Hall. The ruin of the Hall is to be found just above the confluence of two streams. The grounds are covered with mixed woodlands and an estimated 40,000 rhododendrons and azaleas planted by the 19th century owners of the Hall.

Follow the path up the more northerly of the two streams. Cross the stream and proceed up the valley. In about a quarter of a mile, there is a signpost pointing up the hillside to the right (marked 2b). Take this path which climbs to Foxlow Edge.

One of the problems with many gritstone hills in the Peak District is that they are so gently rounded that the views from their tops are uninteresting. Foxlow Edge is sufficiently steep on both sides to give excellent views over the surrounding countryside. From here, the full extent of the Goyt catchment area can be appreciated (and its obvious attraction to municipal water engineers).

From Foxlow Edge, descend to rejoin the main path coming up the valley. (The shrine built by the Grimshawe family of Errwood Hall in memory of their family Governess is a short distance back down the valley from here).

When the path reaches a minor road, turn right and follow it down to the reservoir. This road, The Street, was a Roman road and, in medieval times, was a saltway between Cheshire and Sheffield.

On reaching the reservoir, take the path down the embankment and cross to the eastern side of the reservoir. Turn left and follow the line of the dismantled Cromford and High Peak Railway. The path is lightly wooded with oak and birch and is most attractive.

At the foot of Fernilee reservoir, take the path down the east bank of the river which passes a water treatment building. About two thirds of a mile below the reservoir, take the footbridge across the river into a wood. The path climbs the hillside to the village of Taxal.

At Taxal, the path goes in front of a row of houses and then down to Whaley Bridge. Cross the Macclesfield to Whaley Bridge road into Reddish Lane. This leads to a path to Toddbrook Reservoir. Cross the top of the reservoir embankment and turn right down Reservoir Road. This will bring you to the Jodrell Arms at the centre of Whaley Bridge. Turn left here to the terminus of the High Peak Canal.

Section 2: Whaley Bridge to Compstall

Distance: 9.6 miles

Starting point: SK011815

Map: 7.2

At the terminus, the path passes the building in which goods were transferred between railway and canal barge and then proceeds down the eastern side of the canal.

About a quarter of a mile after the Whaley Bridge canal terminus, the canal spur to Bugsworth is reached which you cross by footbridge. Notice on the eastern side of the valley the extensive brick railway embankment. With its shales and glacial deposits, the Goyt valley has on a number of occasions presented great problems to the civil engineers.

From the Bugsworth spur, follow the canal path for about a mile and a half until a path is reached which goes down to the river. Cross a bridge and follow the river to the gritstone gorge at New Mills known as the Torrs. As you enter the Torrs, the path follows the line of an old mill leat under the Church Road bridge (built 1835) to meet the River Sett. (The path to the right leads to the Sett Valley Trail which follows the line of the dismantled New Mills to Hayfield railway).

Cross the Sett and take the path along the east side of the Goyt under another bridge. After passing this bridge, take the steep steps to the right which climb up the side of the Torrs to the centre of New Mills. The Heritage Centre is at the top of these steps and has an interesting display of the history of New Mills.

The Torrs, New Mills

From the Heritage Centre, take the road down to the railway station and cross the railway line. Follow the path down to the river and along the riverbank through Mouseley Wood. Take the path which climbs to the right through a wood to Hague Bar where you cross the Marple to New Mills road (notice the old tollhouse at the cross road). Until the coming of the turnpike in 1801, the only road here was the path you are now following up the hillside.

A short steep climb takes you past Hague Fold Farm to higher ground, where there are good views over the valley below. (Lyme Park may just be seen over the hilltop).

You will join the road coming up from New Mills just before reaching the hamlet of Brook Bottom. Turn left here, just in front of the Fox Inn, onto a path back down to the valley. This path follows a ridge between the Goyt valley on the left and a pleasant wooded valley on the right.

On reaching the railway, take the road under the line next to Strines station. Turn right at the bottom of an incline of setts (Strines Hall is to your left here) along a farm track which goes under the railway line again. When some buildings are reached, ignore the first footpath to the right and, after the road has curved to the right, take the path to the left.

The path now proceeds on the east of the railway line for about half a mile before again passing under the railway line. (This underpass is a much grander affair than the previous ones). After the railway, follow the path down to and along the riverbank.

At the curve in the river beneath Strawberry Hill a fine 18th century packhorse bridge spans the river (Roman Bridge). There is a weir across the river at the foot of the next railway bridge. This weir takes water to the Roman Lakes, originally constructed to power downstream cotton mills, but now used for recreation.

After the second lake, take the bridge across the river and the path into the woods which starts near the bridge. The steepish climb crosses in turn the railway, road and canal. At the canal, turn right to follow the towpath down to Marple where the junction with the Macclesfield canal is reached. The canal now falls over the next mile through a flight of 16 locks.

Although the walk leaves the canal towpath just after lock 2 to proceed to Compstall, it is worth following the towpath for the short distance to the aqueduct which spans the Goyt. At 80 feet above the river, this aqueduct, built in 1800, affords some splendid views.

Retrace your steps to lock 2 and take the path down through the woods to Brabyn Park below. Turn left to reach the river and then right to follow the Goyt upstream to its confluence with the Etherow. At the confluence, there is a cast iron bridge built in 1813 which you cross.

Follow the path ahead until it reaches a road where you turn left down the hill. At the bottom of the hill, cross the river, pass the Compstall Mill and then turn right into the Etherow Country Park where there is a car park.

Places of interest in the Goyt valley

7.1 Buxworth

Originally named Bugsworth after a local family called Bugge, the village was "gentrified" to Buxworth following a campaign by the Vicar.

The Peak Forest canal came to Bugsworth in 1797 and its terminus is still known as Bugsworth (rather that Buxworth) basin. Here limestone brought down from the Dove Hole Quarry was processed in kilns and transshipped. The tramway was closed in 1925.

In 1866 a landslip caused the Midland Railway line through Bugsworth to collapse. The line was resited further uphill and a massive brick retaining wall built.

7.2 Compstall

(see Etherow valley 6.1)

7.3 Cromford and High Peak Railway

Originally a canal was planned to cross the Peak District connecting the Cromford and Peak Forest canals. The plan failed due to the lack of water but was resurrected with the advent of railways.

The railway was designed by canal engineers and, like a canal, was built as a series of flat sections connected by steep inclines.

Carriages were pulled up the inclines using stationery engines. On the flat sections horses were initially used until displaced by steam locomotives.

The railway was opened in 1830 and, although the section north of Ladmanlow was abandoned in 1894 (when a quicker alternative route which did not use inclines became available), the southern section remained in service until 1967. Goods took two days to cover the 33 miles from Cromford to Whaley Bridge and some trains carried passengers until 1877, when the practice was discontinued following a fatality.

When the Errwood reservoir was created, a road across the valley was lost and an alternative route down the hillside was built on the Bunsal Cob Incline. The small reservoir at the top of this incline was the water supply for the stationary engines.

Much of the former railway track has been incorporated into footpaths, including the inclines used on the Derwent valley walk and the path down the eastern side of Fernilee.

7.4 Errwood Hall

The wealthy Grimshawe family were the major landowners in the upper Goyt valley in the 19th century. The Hall was given to Samuel Grimshawe by his father as a wedding present in 1830 and remained in the family until 1930. The Hall operated on a splendid scale with 20 staff, a resident priest, a private school for 30 children and its own coal mine. The shrine below Foxlow Edge is in memory of the Spanish aristocratic lady who was the family governess.

The Hall was demolished when the Errwood Reservoir was built and is today a ruin amongst the rhododendrons, azaleas and pine-woods planted by the Grimshawe family.

7.5 Goyt Reservoirs

The Fernilee (1938) and Errwood (1969) reservoirs, each with a capacity of about 1000 million gallons, were built to provide 7-8 million gallons a day of drinking water to Stockport.

The packhorse bridge on the road which was inundated by the Errwood reservoir was re-erected upstream where it may be seen at

Goytsclough Quarry. This route across the Goyt was on the line of a Roman Road from Buxton (probably to the Cheshire saltfields). In medieval times it was also used as a saltway from Cheshire to Sheffield. This is the route which crossed the Derwent valley via Curbar Gap (see Derwent valley walk).

7.6 Goytsclough Quarries

In the 17th century, the quarry produced paving slabs which the owner, Thomas Pickford, delivered to London using a team of packhorses. On the return journey the packhorses brought London goods back to Derbyshire, thus establishing Pickfords, the well-known transport Company.

Goyt Bridge, which crosses the river near the quarry, is also of the 17th century. Previously it stood on one of the medieval saltways which crossed the Goyt further down the valley and was re-erected at Goytsclough when the Errwood Reservoir was inundated.

7.7 Marple

At Marple, the High Peak Canal descends a flight of 16 locks to the valley below where it crosses an aqueduct 80 feet above the River Goyt. The canal tollhouse faces lock 16 and there is a 3 storey warehouse (now offices) at lock 10.

Marple Hall was the birth place of Marple's most (in)famous son. Judge Bradshaw sentenced Charles the First to death. Following his own death in the plague, the Judge was buried in ceremony in Westminster Abbey. However, on the restoration of the monarchy, Charles the Second had the Judge's body dug up and hung at Tyburn.

7.8 New Mills

New Mills takes its name not from the cotton mills for which it became famous in the 19th century but rather from a corn mill established on the River Sett in 1391. The town however was a slow starter and was not finally established from its component villages until the late 19th century.

With the invention by Arkwright of water-powered cotton spinning in the late 18th century, the Torrs of New Mills developed rapidly as a cotton centre. The Torrs, a 90 feet deep gorge through the gritstone, was the result of the River Goyt being diverted by a glacial moraine deposited across the former river channel.

Despite the growth of textile production, the Torrs remained a major obstacle to transport in New Mills until 1884 when the last bridge was built to connect the villages and allow the formation of a single parish. A consequence of the high cost of building turnpikes in the Goyt valley was that the Turnpike Trusts erected a large number of tollbars around New Mills. These were extremely unpopular with the inhabitants and led to rioting in 1836 and 1837.

Today, New Mills is a bustling town which makes sweets rather than cotton. After many years of dereliction, the Torrs has been opened and attracts visitors on the Goyt Way and Sett Valley Trail. The Heritage Centre showing the history of the town and area is well worth a visit.

7.9 Taxal

This small hamlet provides the Parish Church, St Leonards, for the much larger (and later established) Whaley Bridge in the valley below.

Whilst mainly Victorian restoration, St Leonards has a 16th century tower. It has numerous memorials to the Jodrells, a local landowning family for 500 years after whom the Cheshire radio-telescope is named. It also has a memorial to Michael Heathcote who had the delightful title of "Gentleman of the Pantry and Yeoman of the Mouth", i.e. foodtaster, to George the Second.

Taxal is on a medieval saltway from Cheshire to Sheffield which crosses the Derwent valley at Stanage (see Derwent valley walk).

Walk 8: The River Hamps

Distance: 12 miles

Ordnance Survey map: Outdoor Leisure 24, The White Peak

Starting point: Mermaid Inn, Morridge SK 037605

The best-known part of this river is between Waterhouses and the confluence with the River Manifold. A popular walk along a converted railway track follows the river as it winds its way along a narrow valley between limestone hills. In the summer, this section of the river is dry.

The upper reaches of the Hamps are less well-known. Here, the softer gritstone and shale leads to rolling hills and panoramic views. While it is possible to walk in close proximity to the river from its source, a more interesting way to start the walk is to the east of the river, along the watershed between the Hamps and the Warslow Brook. There are particularly fine views from a trig point above Upper Elkstone.

In addition to the converted railway line, the walk includes sections along former packhorse routes which were used to take copper ore to the smelters, and an early medieval road known as Earl's Way.

Limestone quarrying has been the main industry around Waterhouses for several centuries. At Waterhouses, the walk passes Brown End Quarry, a geological Nature Reserve of national importance.

Although the Hamps walk is described as a single walk from source to just after its confluence with the Manifold, it may easily be divided into shorter sections. The car park at Waterhouses is very conveniently situated for this purpose. Alternatively, a circular walk could be made by adding a section between Weags Bridge and Ford through Grindon. Grindon would make a good starting point for the circular walk.

The Hamps at Onecote

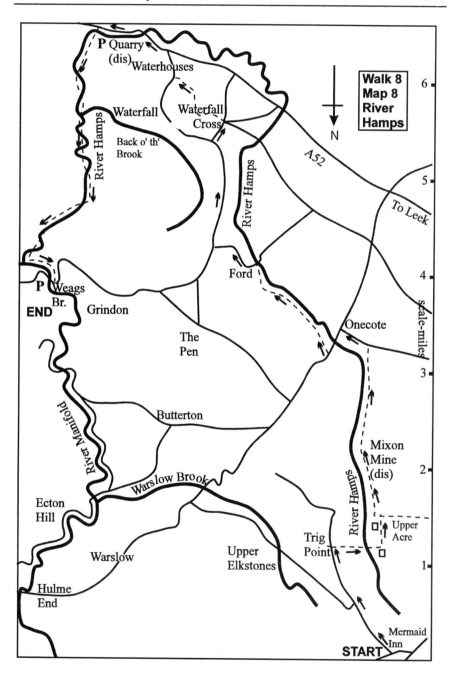

The Walk

The Mermaid Inn on Morridge is the starting point for both the Hamps and the Churnet walks. Car parking at the Inn is reserved for patrons, but there is a limited amount of roadside parking opposite.

From the Mermaid Inn, first take the road towards Warslow, but shortly turn right towards Upper Elkstone. In just under a mile from the Mermaid, when the road to Upper Elkstone bears left, keep to the road going straight on which follows the line of the Hamps.

In a further three quarters of a mile, you will come to a place where there are footpath signs both to the left and right of the road. Although it is the path to the right which you will soon take, you should initially bear left to climb the short distance to the trig point above you. From here there are marvellous views across the Warslow Brook to the limestone hills of the Manifold and the Dove valley beyond. You are standing on the edge of an area of limestone, looking down over the shales to the limestone beyond. The shales, being softer than the limestones, have been preferentially eroded. It is this combination of the low shale basin and the higher limestone hills which creates the wonderful view.

To the south east, you will see the church spires of Butterton and Grindon. The end of the Hamps walks is at Weags Bridge just beyond Grindon, after a walk which includes nearly all points of the compass.

From the trig point, now turn west and follow the path down to the Hamps. Cross the small footbridge and climb the field until you are level with a farm. Although not signposted, a public footpath bears left here towards the next farm down the valley, Upper Acre. The path skirts the top side of Upper Acre, and, in a short distance, you will reach a signpost which points towards the river. Before the river is reached, the path swings right, and you follow a line of stiles across the fields to the site of the former Mixon copper mine.

On the way to the mine, you will cross over an area where there was a dam. You will see another dam across the Hamps. Unlike the Ecton copper mine on the Manifold, the Mixon mine was plagued by ingress of water. The dams are associated with the pumping engines which had to be installed to keep the mine dry.

At the mine, the spoil tips have been levelled to produce a small landing strip. The footpath crosses this area and, if you look very carefully, you may be able to see small samples of copper ore in the spoil.

From the mine, follow the track down the west side of the river to Onecote. This is a rather better track than those further up the river, and was originally the packhorse route used to take the copper out of the mine for processing at Whiston (see Churnet valley walk).

Onecote is one of the few settlements in the Hamps valley, and has a popular pub, The Jervis Arms, on the riverbank. At Onecote take the road through the village towards Warslow. In the second field after the river, you will come to a footpath sign to the right. Take this, and follow the river downstream.

In just over half a mile, the footpath joins a farm track for a short distance. Just before the farm track crosses the river, the footpath bears left to keep to the east side of the river down to the hamlet of Ford.

There are some fine buildings at Ford by the side of the Hamps and here you should take the road which climbs upwards towards Grindon. After a climb of about 200 feet, leave the Grindon road, turning south to follow a road which runs parallel to the Hamps. There are good views looking to your right down the Hamps valley, and also to you left down a small valley which runs to Back o' th' Brook. You are now following the old packhorse route used to take the copper ore from the Ecton mine to the Churnet for processing. If you look on the map you will see "The Pen" marked to the north. This was the storage depot used by the packhorsemen.

When you reach the point where there is a turning to the right, you should take this road to bring you to Waterfall Cross.

This is a crossing point of some antiquity. In early medieval times, the road coming from the west over the river was known as the Earl's Way. This was the route taken by the Earl of Chester's men when visiting the Earl's extensive Staffordshire landholdings. (This is the same Earl's Way which passes the south side of Bosley Cloud on the Dane valley walk).

If you look to the west, you will see a line of trees climbing up the hillside on the other side of the River Hamps. Although not now a road, this was the original line to the west of Earl's Way. From

Waterfall Cross, take the Earl's Way in the other direction towards
the south east and Waterhouses.

At Waterhouses, you will meet the A52 which you should follow
through the village. The River Hamps is at the side of the road in
the winter. In summer the riverbed is dry, the river having disappeared underground only to reappear downstream at Ilam Hall.

Just before the Hamps turns north, there is a car park at the side
of the road. Behind this car park is a quarry which has been
converted into a nature reserve by the Staffordshire Wild Life Trust.
Here, the limestone strata are almost vertical, allowing you to walk
through time as you move along the quarry face. Perhaps the most
fascinating evidence in the rocks is of turbidity currents – essentially
fossilised earthquakes!

Next to the car park you come to a building where, if you are so
minded, you may hire a cycle for use on the Manifold Trail. Waterhouses was the terminus of the Leek and Manifold Valley Light
Railway. The track has now been converted into a path and cycle
track which will take you all the way to Hulme End.

Like the Manifold, the Hamps is sinuous as it runs through the
limestone, and the railway line constantly crosses and recrosses the
river on its journey to the Manifold.

You will reach the Manifold in about two and a half miles from
Waterhouses at Beeston Tor. Here, you should continue to follow
the railway track for another half a mile before coming to a car park
at Weags Bridge.

Walk 9: Rivers Lathkill and Bradford

Distance: 10.5 miles

Ordnance Survey map: Outdoor Leisure 24, The White Peak

Starting point: SK 157665

Although much of the Peak District has lost its floral diversity after centuries of agricultural "improvement", a few places have remained untouched. One such very special place is the Lathkill valley, recognised because of its flora as a National Nature Reserve. In the Upper Lathkill, over 50 species of plant have been recorded in a single square metre.

As well as the flowers, some of which are nationally rare, the valley has ashwoods, dating back to Anglo-Saxon times, which are amongst some of the oldest in the country. The wide variety of flora provides a diverse food source for butterflies, with some twenty species breeding in the valley.

The Lathkill and Bradford rivers are almost unique in the country in flowing entirely on limestone and producing a water quality which supports crayfish and the formation of an unusual mineral called "tufa".

Charles Cotton, co-author with Izaac Walton of "The Compleat Angler", called the Lathkill "... the purest and most transparent stream I ever saw ... with the reddest trouts in England". A scenic feature of both rivers is the large number of weirs and pools built to improve the fishing.

There is evidence that the valleys were inhabited in the Bronze Age and, within a short distance of the two rivers, there are a number of important archeological sites including Arbor Low and Benty Grange. This archeological richness was no doubt the stimulus for the local Victorian, Thomas Bateman, who excavated so many of the Peak District pre-historic sites. Much of the material from his digs is to be seen in the Sheffield Museum.

The Danes must have occupied the valley, for Lathkill is a Norse name meaning "narrow valley with a barn". The mainstay of the valley's economy for several centuries was lead mining. A number of remains from the mining period may be seen on the walk.

The circular walk is mainly along the bottom of the two river valleys with a short linking section between them over the limestone plateau above.

Pool in upper Lathkill Dale

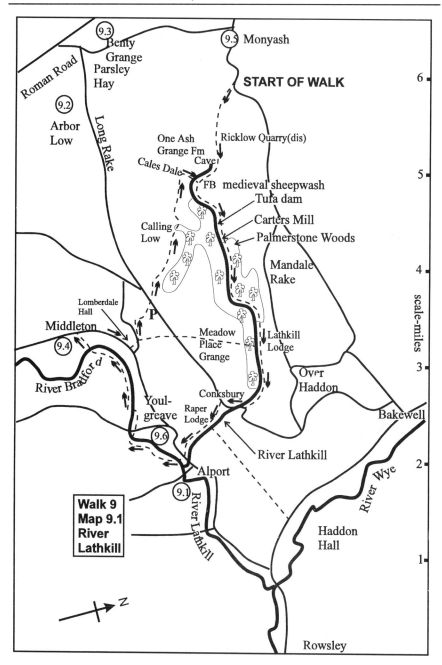

The Walk

Lathkill Dale is perhaps best reached from the Monyash to Bakewell Road just to the east of Monyash. A slight dip in the road as it crosses the top of the dry valley signals the Lathkill. There is parking here at the roadside.

For the first couple of fields below the road, the path follows the bottom of a shallow depression. On entering the third field, there are limestone escarpments on both sides.

Shortly, the path reaches a fall of limestone boulders which almost blocks the way. This is not a natural fall, but rather the debris from a former quarry. Ricklow Quarry produced a dark limestone which took a high polish to produce "Ashford Marble", used in many stately homes including Chatsworth.

After the quarry, the valley widens and the limestone outcrops are now high above. It was from one of these pinnacles that the Vicar of Monyash fell from his horse to his death in 1766. Thereafter the pinnacle became known as Parson's Tor.

As the valley turns to the right, a cave is reached which is the winter source of the river. In summer, the source is further downstream.

Just before reaching Cales Dale, there are carpets of thyme at the bottom of the scree slopes. If not in flower, thyme may be recognized by its aroma when squeezed between the fingers. In dry summers, drought resistant herbs such as the thyme are an important source of nectar for the dales butterflies.

There is a footbridge at the junction with Cales Dale. Here, there is the remains of a medieval sheepwash first used by the monks of One Ash Grange in the 12th and 13th centuries.

At Cales Dale, the southern side of the valley changes from limestone grassland to ancient woodland. It is believed that these woodlands have been largely undisturbed since Anglo-Saxon times. The northern slopes remain unwooded for another half a mile. The hillside grassland is grazed in rotation. Whilst the grazing animals temporarily remove the flowers, they permanently inhibit the growth of tree cover. If the ground were left ungrazed, woodland would soon establish itself and crowd out all the grassland flowers.

About half a mile below Cales Dale, look out for a dam made of tufa. Tufa is an extremely unusual form of calcium carbonate, deposited as a result of the interaction between carbonate bearing water, algae, moss and bacteria.

The woods are reached on the northern side of the valley at Palmerstone Woods. Unlike the ancient woodland on the southern slopes, this woodland is relatively modern, having become established only after lead mining ceased in the mid 19th century.

Just before the woods, there is a large mill pool where, until the Second World War, corn was ground at Carters Mill. Of the Mill only a few stones remain, but if you search the undergrowth at the foot of the pool on the northern bank you will see two millstones.

With woodlands on both sides of the valley, the pathway now becomes a tunnel under a high canopy. This impression of enclosure is at its greatest in late summer when the riverside vegetation is higher than head height, and in places obscures the view of the river.

At Mandale Rake, there are limestone pillars across the river. This was an important lead mining area. At the end of the 18th century the mine workings had reached such a depth that a "sough" was required to carry the water out of the mine to the river. This sough, which took several years to cut, is over a mile long. By 1839 the sough on its own was unable to dewater the mine and one of the largest waterwheels in the country was installed. The limestone pillars carried the water across the river to the wheel.

By taking a slight detour into the woods at the left by the limestone pillars, you may follow the old mill leat before coming to a mine entrance, the pit for the waterwheel and the shell of an old engine house. From the engine house descend to the river. Rejoin the path, keeping a look out for the sough bringing the water out of the mine (at the side of the path).

When Lathkill Lodge is reached there is a path to the left to Over Haddon. Meadow Place Grange, the site of a monastic grange belonging to the monks of Leicester Abbey, is to the right across the river. For those interested in fossils, the limestone slabs of the footbridge have some good sized crinoids.

Take neither of these paths, but carry on down the river. In this area, not all the rocks are limestone. An intrusion of volcanic material is seen on the immediate left at the side of the path.

In the summer, the river is usually dry here; the riverbed overgrown with vegetation. The path climbs over a small limestone outcrop and the river reappears, now as a series of attractive pools built in the 19th century to improve the fishing. The pools do tend to be rather choked with weed in summer, but there is a clear area at the top of each pool where the velocity is highest. In these regions you will see the trout admired by Charles Cotton.

A series of eleven pools takes you down to Conksbury bridge, where you cross the river. From the bridge it is often possible to see the trout at close quarters. After the bridge, follow the road uphill for a short distance until reaching a footpath leading off to the left. Take this and, in a third of a mile, Raper Lodge is reached. In 1944 chert and flint implements were found in a small cave in the grounds of Raper Lodge. These are thought to be of Bronze Age and to confirm that the Lathkill was settled at that time.

A path across the packhorse bridge below Raper Lodge leads towards the River Wye (Haddon Hall and Bakewell). Below Raper Lodge you are in a lovely open valley with mature deciduous trees on the other side of the river, which display a great variety of colours in summer.

The Lathkill and Bradford meet in a delightful meadowland setting at Alport. The Lathkill tumbles down a series of small rapids with the 17th and 18th century houses of Alport village behind.

From the junction of the two rivers the path follows the Bradford upstream. After crossing the river there is a white gate with a splendid delatching mechanism. Not only are the ironwork fittings a work of art, but the mechanism allows the gate to be opened with only a few ounces of pressure. A Rolls Royce of a gate.

Soon Youlgreave is on the skyline above and is well worth a visit. The path crosses from left bank to right bank and passes a series of pools popular with both the cattle and the local children.

The path crosses back again over a stone clapper bridge into the Haddon Estate, with a series of finely-built 19th century dams. Again, some of these hold good trout.

Bradford Dale

The valley bears left before a sign is reached indicating that the Limestone Way is to the right. Do not take this path but carry on up the river for about a fifth of a mile before bearing right uphill into Middleton.

There are three wells in Middleton (dressed in May) and Thomas Bateman the Victorian archeologist arranged for them to be fed from a pumping station in Bradford dale. His initials, TWB, are engraved on the wells.

As you take the road out of Middleton towards Youlgreave, you pass the former Congregational church built by Bateman. His tomb is behind the church. A further third of a mile down the road you come to the house where Bateman lived; Lomberdale Hall.

Almost immediately after the Hall, there is a path bearing left diagonally up the field which you take. At the top of the field a road is reached. Directly across the road is a path which would take you to Lathkill Lodge. Ignore this path, turn left up the road and then take the path into the field on the right which climbs steeply up the field towards the edge of a wood. At the top of the field bear right and follow the track to the car park on the Parsley Hay to Conksbury road.

On the way to the car park there are extensive views to the east over the Lathkill, the Wye and the Derwent. On a clear day a row of cottages may be seen on the Derwent. These are the cottages built for the railway workers at Rowsley.

After the car park, the path crosses the Parsley Hay to Conksbury Road and then proceeds across the fields. Looking back, you can see mining operations being carried out in the woods along Long Rake. The mine is extracting calcite, a material often associated with lead.

The path ahead is well used and easy to follow. It goes through a small wood before skirting the farm at Calling Low. It is easy to understand, in crossing the high limestone plateau, why it is so little populated. There are no obvious sources of water.

At Calling Low, the path begins to descend to the valley. One Ash Grange, originally a medieval farm belonging to the monks of Roche Abbey, may be seen at the other side of Cales Dale.

When Cales Dale is reached, the path descends somewhat precipitously down the steps to the valley floor. At the bottom, the path to the right takes you back to the Lathkill, and then up the valley to Monyash.

Places of interest in the Lathkill and Bradford Valleys

9.1 Alport

Most of the houses in this delightful village are from the 17th and 18th century and the mill and bridge are of the 18th century. The village, however, is much older. Even in the Saxon period, when the village was named after the portway that ran through it, the Saxons indicated in using the prefix "Al" (old) that the route was then ancient.

Alport was a lead mining area which, by the end of the 18th century, was running into problems because of water. To de-water his mines, the Duke of Rutland had a four mile sough driven to the river Derwent just above Darley Dale (Hillcar Sough). The sough took twenty-one years to complete and, to recover its cost, miners were required to pay the Duke a levy on all lead mined below a certain level.

In 1881, a large chasm appeared in the bottom of the River Bradford and the river disappeared underground for several years. What had happened was that the river water had broken into underground lead mine workings and travelled by the Hillcar Sough to the Derwent. Only after the sealing of the chasm was the River Bradford restored.

9.2 Arbor Low

With its 250 feet diameter bank and 50 stones (now recumbent but originally standing), Arbor Low is England's third largest henge after Stonehenge and Avesbury.

The henge has been dated to about 2000BC, and an estimated one million man hours were involved in its construction. This tells us that the inhabitants of the Peak District must have had a sophisticated social structure.

Arbor Low's function can only be guessed. An excavation of 1902/3 has perhaps reinforced the prejudices of those who would like to discover a sinister purpose. A skeleton found during the excavation was not accompanied by the usual grave goods. This, it has been argued, is indicative of a human sacrifice.

9.3 Benty Grange

Following the Roman withdrawal from Britain, the Anglo-Saxons settled the south and east of England but took a considerable time to make their presence felt in the Peak District.

One of the earliest traces of their penetration into the region was found when Thomas Bateman of Middleton investigated the tumulus at Benty Grange. The tumulus contained a highly unusual helmet with both Christian and pagan symbols (a cross and a bronze boar). A reconstruction of the helmet is to be seen in the Sheffield Museum.

The grave is dated to the 7th century and is thought to be of a warrior. It is known that in the 7th century the West Saxons and

Mercians combined to fight the Northumbrians and that some of the action took place in the Peak District. The two helmet ornaments are consistent with the fact that Mercia only converted to Christianity in AD653. The wearer was possibly backing two horses by seeking the protection of more than one deity!

The juxtaposition of the grave and the old Roman road suggests that the road was still then in use.

9.4 Middleton by Youlgreave

This leafy village was a royalist stronghold in the 17th century. Sir Christopher Fulwood recruited an army of 1000 to fight Cromwell, but was caught and shot in Bradford Dale.

In the 19th century, Middleton was the home of the archeologist Thomas Bateman who excavated some 400 barrows in the Peak District (including four in one day). Many of the artefacts he found are now to be seen in the Sheffield Museum.

Bateman's home was Lomberdale Hall and he built the Congregational Chapel in Middleton (his tomb is in the grounds) and also installed a water system to Middleton's three wells, water being pumped from the river below.

9.5 Monyash ("many ashes")

Lack of a water supply is the reason for there being so few villages on the limestone plateau. It was only possible to establish a village at Monyash because a number of small streams flow off a clay deposit and were collected in five ponds. Today only one of these remains.

The village existed in Norman times (there is some Norman architecture in the church) and was the early recipient of a market charter (1340). The market cross stands on the green next to the inn.

In the 18th century, Monyash was a Quaker stronghold, the Meeting House now being a Youth Centre.

In 1776, the Monyash vicar fell from his horse to his death in Lathkill Dale. The pinnacle from which he fell is known as Parson's Tor.

The Chandler's House is where candles were made for the lead mining industry and the lead mining court, the Barmote, still meets in Monyash.

9.6 Youlgreave ("old mine")

Youlgreave is famous for its June Well Dressing which started in 1829 in celebration of the first water supply to the village. The cylindrical conduit for this supply holds 1200 gallons.

The church is one of the finest in the Peak District. It has some fabric from Norman times, together with considerable later additions from the 14th and 19th centuries. It has some very fine artefacts which include a Norman font of an unusual design, the tomb chest of Thomas Cokayne, an alabaster commemorating the family of Richard Gilbert (17 children) and a 14th century knight holding a heart in his hands (thought to be that of Robert the Bruce).

The attractive Old Hall is dated 1656 and the Bull's Head is a 16th century Coaching Inn. The Co-op, now a Youth Hostel, was used in the filming of "The Virgin and the Gypsy".

Walk 10: River Manifold

Distances:

Total: 18.6 miles

Section 1: Axe Edge to Hulme End: 9.8 miles

Section 2: Hulme End to Ilam: 8.8 miles

Ordnance Survey map: Outdoor Leisure 24, The White Peak

The Manifold is perhaps best-known as one of the Peak District rivers which disappears in summer for part of its length. Although the upper half of the Manifold is little walked, the whole of this river valley, from its source on Axe Edge to its confluence with the Dove, is a superb walking area. The valley is one of two contrasting halves:

- ¤ from its source on Axe Edge to Hulme End the underlying rocks are gritstones and shales giving rise to rolling hills, broad panoramic views and a moorland flora
- ¤ at Hulme End the limestone is reached and, down to the confluence with the Dove, the river twists in a narrow valley between limestone hills. This limestone area is particularly floriferous with an abundance of flowers typical of northern limestone country – orchids, rockroses, water avens, violets, saxifrage and the wild strawberry

Remains from Thor's Cave show that the lower valley attracted settlers shortly after the last Ice Age, and an Anglo-Saxon hoard of treasure found at Beeston Tor suggests that the Vikings colonised the valley in the AD870s. This colonisation is also confirmed by some of the few place names of Danish origin in the Peak District.

During the 18th and early 19th centuries the copper mine at Ecton made the Manifold one of the power houses of the early Industrial Revolution. Former packhorse routes and the converted Leek and Manifold Valley Light Railway make the Manifold extremely well provided with footpaths. It is also well supplied throughout its length with adequate car parking, allowing a good variety of different types and lengths of walk to be selected.

River resurgence at Ilam

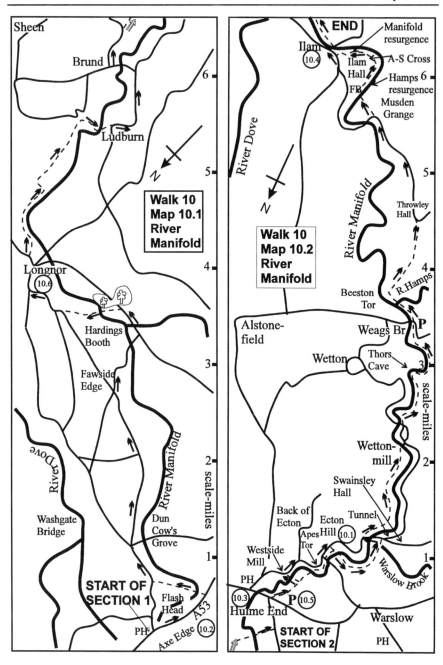

The Walk

Section 1: Axe Edge to Hulme End

Distance: 9.8 miles

Starting point: SK031678

Map: 10.1

Axe Edge, just to the south west of Buxton, is the source of several of the rivers featured in this book – the Dove, Manifold, Goyt, Dane and Churnet. The Manifold itself rises at Flash Head, in the field below the Travellers Rest public house on the A53.

From the public house, follow the A53 away from Buxton towards Leek. The Manifold is to the left, whilst ahead the craggy gritstone outcrop of the Roaches may be seen in the distance. The A53 is on the line of an old Roman Road which fell out of use for many centuries until the turnpike from Leek to Buxton was built in the 1770s. Despite being a busy main road, it is safe to walk here because of its broad grass verge.

After a few minutes, a signpost is passed pointing towards Flash, the highest village in England. A little further down the A53 two paths cross the road. Like so many of the footpaths and bridleways in the Dove and Manifold valleys, these are medieval packhorse ways.

Take the path to the left which descends to the valley bottom. Notice how, after such a short distance from its source, the river has already cut a deep incision. The steepness of the hillside means that the busy road above quickly becomes inaudible. Crossing the river, the path ahead is typical of old packhorse roads, cutting into the hillside as it winds upwards.

Follow the path over the brow of the hill to meet a broader path from the left. After the farmhouse do not follow the main path which climbs to the left, but take a line diagonally across the field to the right. The only indication that this is indeed a footpath is a stile at the other side of the field. A track is met at the other side of the next field, where there is a good show of primroses in the spring.

Keeping to the track, a barn and then a farm are passed before the road descending from the Travellers Rest is joined. This road along the edge top is followed for approximately two miles and gives a succession of delightful views

¤ to the right, the River Manifold runs at the bottom of the gritstone edge, with the broad panorama of the Manifold catchment area behind, stretching away to the horizon

¤ ahead is the gritstone ridge with the limestone hills behind

¤ to the left are the limestone reef knolls of the Dove valley.

The first minor road met, going down to Dun Cow's Grove, was originally a packhorse route from Cheshire to Derbyshire and Nottinghamshire. Immediately to the west of the river may be seen the hollow-way of this packhorse route ascending the moorside. (This packhorse route is also seen on the River Dove walk at the lovely Washgate packhorse bridge).

About two miles after joining the road and, just before reaching the hamlet of Fawside Edge, take the minor road to the right which descends to the river at Hardings Booth. The road meets the river at a ford and footbridge and here the valley changes its character. Above the ford the valley is narrow. Below, the valley widens to perhaps half a mile. This is the first fertile area met since leaving Axe Edge.

Bear left towards Longnor, crossing the stream coming down off Morridge to join the Manifold. The road climbs uphill and, just before a wood, take the gate across a cattlegrid into the field on the left. Again, there is no indication that this a right of way until a footbridge is reached at the river. Go through the farm ahead, Fawside, before joining the road which leads to Longnor with its wide Market Square, Market Hall and Coaching Inn.

Leaving Longnor Market Square towards Crowdecote, you shortly reach Folds End Farm on the right. Take the path through the farm. When the path divides, take the lower branch down to the river. From here down to Hulme End there is a broad alluvial valley bottom. The farms are all set well away from the river on the rising land since the valley is liable to flooding.

Several farms in this area have Booth in their title, suggesting use for cattle raising perhaps stretching back to the time of the Danish occupation. (Booth is a Norse word for cowshelter).

About a mile and a half from Longnor, take a path to the right down to the river. This again is a packhorse road which forded the river at Ludburn, hollow-ways indicating its ancient usage.

Cross the footbridge and then turn left to join the minor road in about a quarter of a mile. Follow this road and, bearing left twice, come to Brund bridge. Until 1891 when the present bridge was built, there was a packhorse bridge here. This was on an ancient saltway, salt being taken from Nantwich to Chesterfield for the glazing of pottery.

The house just across the bridge was previously a mill which sported a 16 foot waterwheel. (There has been a watermill at Brund since the 13th century).

The road ahead shortly comes to a T-junction and the right fork leads towards Brund which has some fine old buildings. About a quarter of a mile after Brund, leave the road and take the path directly ahead. As you cross the fields the view is of a broad valley and, to the south, the narrow passage taken by the river through the limestone hills.

Three fields after leaving the road, you come to a path leading down to the river. From the river, take the path ahead and, on reaching the road, bear left to Hulme End. Both the walls and the buildings are now a mixture of limestone and sandstone confirming that you are at the junction between two different types of rocks.

Geology maps show the alluvial plain terminating at Hulme End. "Hulme" is Danish for watermeadow, suggesting that the Danes established a village here at the edge of the watermeadow. It can be no coincidence that one of the few medieval drove roads through the Peak District also came through Hulme End; the Danes and the drovers, almost a millennium apart, being attracted by the fodder the watermeadows offered their cattle.

Section 2: Hulme End to Ilam

Distance: 8.8 miles

Starting point: SK104593

Map: 10.2

On entering the village of Hulme End, turn right and then almost immediately left into a car park. Between 1904 and 1934 this was the terminus for the Leek and Manifold Valley Light Railway which ran down the Manifold and Hamps valleys to Waterhouses. The sheds on the left are the former booking office and engine shed. The railway track has now been converted to a most attractive path and cycle track.

Follow this track out of the car park. In a few hundred yards, cross the field on the left to the footbridge at Westside Mill. After rain, the field is often heavily waterlogged and it is then necessary to proceed a little further down the railway track before cutting back to cross the footbridge. Notice the pipes being used as a climber for flowers on the river side of the road at Westside Mill. These pipes were originally installed underground in the Ecton Copper Mine.

From the Mill, follow the river down the valley.

When visibility is good, the views from the top of Ecton Hill are some of the best in the Peak District, with vistas over much of the Manifold and Dove valleys. If you wish to take a detour to the top of Ecton Hill, you should take the minor road to the left signed to Back of Ecton. From this road a path to the right leads to the top of the hill.

(There are footpaths across the western face of Ecton Hill which may be used in dry weather. These should be avoided in wet or frosty weather. The hillside is steep and can be dangerously slippery. As in all mining areas, you should keep to the paths and not climb over the mine workings. Some of the shafts drop many hundreds of feet into the hillside!)

Just after the sign to Back of Ecton the limestone outcrop of Apes Tor is reached. Had you been at this spot some 200 years ago you would have seen a horse-drawn whim standing on the flat platform above the mine adit and a stilted aqueduct taking water across the river and into the mine to work the machinery.

The area around Apes Tor and the adjacent fields is particularly floriferous, with a good show of several types of Orchids and other lime loving plants in the summer. In the winter the mosses on the wall-tops have interesting cup like structures.

A little further down the river, the house on the left of the roadside was originally the Mine Manager's. Take the path to the right immediately after the house to rejoin the old railway track.

Few plants are able to grow on the crushed limestone area by the river because of the metal contamination left over from the mining operations. Three plants which do not appear to mind these contaminants, and are to be found on the limestone here, are the saxifrage, the violet and the diminutive leadwort.

It is worth looking over the river bridge to see whether the trout and grayling are active. For a short period at the end of May and the beginning of June there is often a good Mayfly hatch here and the trout abandon their usual caution.

Having crossed the river, follow the railway track downstream for about half a mile before reaching a road just after crossing the Warslow Brook. Here you could continue to follow the line of the old railway through the tunnel (which is used also by vehicles), but a quieter and preferable route is to cross the river and take the gated road on the east side of the river.

To your right, on the hilltop in a most attractive position above the tunnel, is Swainsley Hall with its views down to the river. The structure by the river in the Swainsley Hall grounds is a dovecot.

The track down the river to Wettonmill is quiet and most attractive. Wettonmmill itself is one of the most popular places on the Manifold, being easily accessible to the motorist, and is often crowded in the summer. It is in this area that the river disappears underground during the summer months, only to reappear several miles downstream at Ilam Hall.

At the Mill, cross the river and follow the old railway track down the river. In about half a mile, Thor's cave is reached high above the river. Remains from this cave showed evidence of man's presence in the Manifold valley shortly after the last Ice Age. It is very worthwhile to make the short steep climb up to Thor's Cave from where there are spectacular views up the valley.

Thor's Cave above a dry riverbed

Rejoining the railway track, the River Hamps is reached in about half a mile. The track goes down the Hamps to Waterhouses but the Manifold walk proceeds ahead.

To the left is the vertical outcrop of Beeston Tor which is very popular with climbers. A Saxon brooch dated to about AD875 was found in a cave here and is now displayed in the British Museum. It is probable that this was hidden by the Saxons when the Danes conquered the area in the AD870s.

The path climbs ahead and, when the fields are reached, evidence may be seen of an ancient hollow-way and strip cultivation to each side. The fields here are large, giving broad open vistas. Perhaps this is one of the best places to get a feeling for what the Peak District must have looked like before the field enclosures of the 17th and 18th centuries.

As the path climbs higher, marvellous panoramic views over large areas of the Peak District unfold. Looking back up the valley you will see in the foreground the church spires of Grindon and Butterton and in the background, from west to east, Morridge, Axe Edge and the limestone reef knolls of Upper Dovedale.

The path ahead passes through a rather sparse line of trees on the skyline and then descends to Throwley Hall. The Old Hall, which is now a ruin, has some fine architectural features and, in its day, must have been extremely impressive. It was owned by the Meverells until the male family line died out in 1626 and was then bought by Izaac Walton's friend, Charles Cotton.

From the Hall, the road descending to the river is unfenced and again there are splendid views of open countryside. There is something very attractive about an unfenced road where the open fields directly abut the roadside.

Just before the river the road swings to the left but you should proceed ahead, following the footpath sign (just below the farm building). Follow the line of stiles across the fields, passing Musden Grange (the site of a medieval monastic holding). Cross the river using the footbridge and turn right towards Illam Hall. The water entering the river on the other bank is not a conventional spring, but rather water from the River Hamps which went underground at Waterhouses.

After the resurgence of the Hamps you will pass an 11th century Anglo-Saxon cross before coming to the resurgence of the River Manifold. This time the water has travelled some four miles underground from Wetton Mill, taking about 24 hours to do so.

Here take the path to the left up to Ilam Hall, where there is an Information Centre.

Amongst the exhibits at the Centre are photographs of the Dove valley both today and also at the beginning of the century. With the exclusion of sheep, much of lower Dovedale has now become heavily wooded and has lost its open aspect. This illustrates how much the appearance of the Peak District would change if, for any reason, sheep farming were to become uneconomic.

Leaving the Hall, take the path past the church to Ilam and cross the river. A path leads down the field to the confluence with the Dove. It is interesting to compare the volume of water in the two rivers which rose so close to each other on Axe Edge. The much larger Manifold reflects its greater catchment area.

Although the Manifold is the larger of the two rivers, the downstream river takes the name of the Dove since it is the county boundary. (A description of the walk downstream from here appears in the River Dove walk).

Places of interest in the Manifold valley

10.1 Ecton Copper Mine

Although worked as early as the 1650s, it was not until the 1760s that the Duke of Devonshire fully exploited the potential of his mine at Ecton. By the end of the 18th century, the mine was the deepest in the world at 1400 feet from the top of Ecton Hill to the lowest level some 700 feet below the river. Perhaps one of the most astonishing features of the mine was that it was so watertight. As may be seen from exposures at Apes Tor, the limestone is extensively folded. Yet, with a sizeable river running 700 feet above the lowest workings, its was only necessary to extract some 40 gallons of water an hour, using a 4HP engine.

Significant technical innovation was required to exploit the mine's potential including:

- ¤ first use of explosives in British mining
- ¤ use of underground boats
- ¤ largest balanced hydraulic pumping engine
- ¤ one of the earliest James Watt rotative steam engines
- ¤ two ropes, 1300 feet in length and 7 inches in maximum diameter. These ropes, which had to be replaced every 8 months at a cost of £100, were manufactured in Leek.

Much of the production, which reached a peak of 4000 tons a year in the 1780s, went into the sheathing of naval vessels (hence the term 'copper bottomed'). The ore was transported by packhorse to Whiston for smelting (see Churnet walk).

No machinery was saved from the mine although there is considerable evidence of the former workings on the hillside and of adits at river level. Very considerable profits were made from the mine by the Duke and it is suggested that these financed the building of the Crescent at Buxton.

10.2 Flash (see Dove walk, 5.4)

10.3 Hulme End

This small village is situated just above the flood plain of the Manifold as it flows out of the shales of the Upper Manifold into the limestone of the Lower Manifold.

Hulme End was probably settled by the Danes in the AD870s, for Hulme is a Norse word for "watermeadow". Even today, the low-lying fields on the alluvial plain flood during periods of heavy rain.

In medieval times, Hulme End was on one of the few drove roads known to have crossed the Peak District. The Danes and the drovers, almost a millennium apart, would have been attracted by the good pastures the "watermeadows" offered their cattle.

In 1904, Hulme End became the terminus for the Leek and Manifold Valley Light Railway. The terminus is now a car park serving the Manifold Way, a footpath and cycle track down the Manifold and Hamps valleys between Hulme End and Waterhouses.

10.4 Ilam

The settlement of the area round Ilam is of some antiquity with:

¤ a church of Anglo-Saxon foundation

¤ the Anglo-Saxons farming the higher ground above the valley

¤ the Danes settling nearby Thorpe

¤ a Cistercian settlement at Musden Grange

¤ Throwley Hall occupied for several centuries by the Meverells until 1640 when it was purchased by Izaac Walton's friend Charles Cotton.

Jesse Watts-Russell bought Ilam Hall and had it remodelled in 1821, but little of his building remains. The estate is now owned by the National Trust and the Hall is a Youth Hostel.

There is an Anglo-Saxon cross in the grounds and, close by at Dunstan Crags, the rivers Manifold and Hamps resurface after travelling underground from respectively Wettonmill and Waterhouses.

10.5 Leek and Manifold Valley Light Railway

In 1898 an Act of Parliament authorised the Leek Light Railway and, in 1904, its narrow gauge section (30 inches) between Waterhouses and Hulme End was opened.

The railway has a tunnel at Swainsley (the result of Sir Thomas Wardle of Swainsley Hall insisting that the line passed under rather than through his grounds) and a number of unusual features:

¤ a transporter to allow standard gauge rolling stock to be piggy-backed

¤ large lamps and cowcatchers on the engines (never used). These "colonial" style features were the result of the railway company employing an engineer whose previous experience had been in India.

The main revenues for the line came from the transport of milk (daily to London) and of day trippers (5000 people were carried on the line one Whit week-end).

Swainsley Hall

The closure of the Ecton Dairy in 1930 made the railway uneconomic and it too closed in 1934. Today, the old railway line is popular as a walking and cycle track, the Manifold Way. There is parking at both ends of the trail and cycles may be hired at Waterhouses. The engine shed and booking office of the old Leek and Manifold Valley Light Railway are still to be seen in the car park at Hulme End.

10.6 Longnor

Longnor is a fine sandstone village built on a slope between the Dove and Manifold rivers. Its position between the two rivers made it a meeting point for several packhorse routes.

The need for large quantities of chert to be transported from the

Wye to the North Staffordshire potteries resulted in 1765 in an Act of Parliament to build a turnpike road through Longnor. One of the turnpike routes from Buxton to London also passed through Longnor, and the Crewe and Harpur Arms is a former Coaching Inn.

The Old Market Hall sports a table of market tolls payable to the Lord of the Manor, Sir Vancy Harpur Crewe,and is now a craft shop specialising in furniture, paintings and jewellery.

Walks 11.1 and 11.2:
River Noe and Peakshole Water

The two valleys provide a number of superb walks which combine sections from both valleys. Although the two walks are described separately, they are brought together in a single chapter to allow the planning of combined walks.

The Edale valley

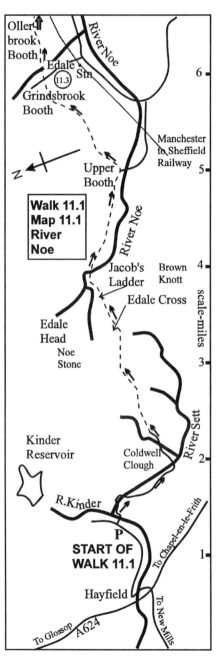

Walk 11.1: River Noe

Distance: 12 miles

Map: Outdoor Leisure 1, The Dark Peak

Starting point: Kinder Bank Car Park, Hayfield SK 048869

Edale has been popular for walking since Victorian times when the opening of the Manchester to Sheffield railway made Edale accessible to the city dweller.

The Noe (meaning "flowing") rises at Edale Head on the southern edge of Kinder Scout and flows eastwards to join the Derwent at Bamford. The landslips along both sides of the valley due to underlying shale.

As there are no roads near the source of the Noe, the walk starts in the adjacent Sett valley and climbs 1000ft to Edale Cross before going steeply down Jacob's Ladder into the Edale valley.

The middle section is along the northern side of the Edale valley with views across to the ridgeway between Mam Tor and Lose Hill. The last section follows the Noe through Hope to the Roman fort of Navio, then along the valley to the junction with the Derwent.

Car parking at Edale makes this a good place to split the walk. A circular walk may be made by joining parts of the Edale and Hope valley walks (e.g. adding a section from Edale to Mam Tor).

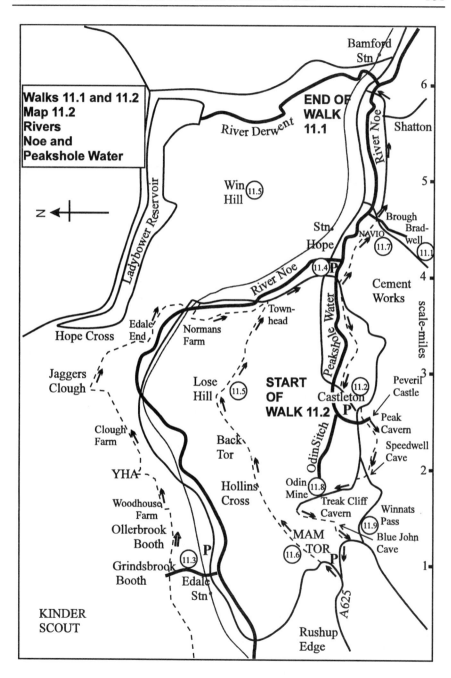

Walks 11.1 and 11.2
Map 11.2
Rivers
Noe and
Peakshole Water

Peakshole Water, Castleton

Walk 11.2: Peakshole Water and Odin Sitch (Hope valley)

Distance: 8 miles

Map: Outdoor Leisure 1, The Dark Peak.

Starting point: Castleton SK 015830

The valley has some spectacular views, particularly from the ancient ridgeway which runs between Mam Tor and Lose Hill. The combination of first class scenery, caves and attractive villages makes the Hope valley a major tourist attraction. It has not been overdeveloped and spoilt as have so many tourist venues, but those wishing to avoid the crowds should time their visits carefully to avoid peak periods.

Daniel Defoe once commented that the whole county of Derbyshire was hollow. Nowhere is this more true than in the adjacent valleys of Hope and Rushup. Surface rivers such as the Peakshole Water and Odin Sitch are small in comparison with their catchment areas and in these valleys the predominant waterflows are subterranean. Many tens of miles of passageways have been explored by potholers.

In addition to the natural underground passageways, there are many more which are the result of Man's search for minerals (possibly as far back as the Roman occupation). The public has access to five caverns which are each different and all worth visiting:

¤ Peak Cavern

¤ Speedwell Cavern

¤ Treak Cliff Cavern

¤ Blue John Cavern

¤ Bagshawe Cavern (Bradwell)

Historically, the Hope valley was of considerable strategic importance as may be seen from the number of ancient fortifications from different periods sited in close proximity to each other:

¤ a major Iron Age hill fort at Mam Tor

¤ a Roman Camp (Navio)

¤ the Norman Peveril Castle perched above Castleton.

The walk described is circular, taking in most of the places of interest in the valley. The suggested starting point is Castleton, since Peveril Castle is a good vantage point from which most of the walk may be viewed. The Peakshole Water is followed on the return journey to Castleton but the Odin Stich is excluded since the alternative more southerly route is of greater interest.

The valley is relatively well-provided with parking. In addition to the car parks in Castleton, Hope and at Mam Tor, parking is allowed on the road out of Castleton towards Winnats Pass and on the cul-de-sac formed by the abandoned road beneath Mam Tor.

The River Noe (Edale Valley) walk (maps 11.1 and 11.2)

The walk starts from the same point as the Ashop Walk, in the car park between Hayfield and the Kinder Reservoir. From the car park, cross the River Sett and follow the river upstream to the confluence with the River Kinder, where there is a lovely packhorse bridge.

Packhorse bridge over the River Kinder at its confluence with the River Sett

After crossing two small bridges, the road first climbs upwards and then descends to recross the river, before turning eastwards up Coldwell Clough. At the top of the first rise above the river, there is a farmhouse with 'E+B 1804' marked over the door.

From the river, a steady climb of about 900 feet and two miles brings you to Edale Cross. Do look back as you climb towards the cross for there are some splendid panoramic views of the hills to the west and south.

Edale Cross is set in a stone alcove by the side of the track and is dated 1810. The Cross is in fact much older than this date mark would suggest, being a medieval boundary marker between monastic lands and the Royal Peak Forest.

As you proceed ahead towards Edale, the southern edge of Kinder Scout comes into view, and the streams tumbling into the valley on your left are the headwaters of the River Noe.

In less than a mile from the Cross you come to the steep descent of Jacob's Ladder, named after an 18th century packhorse man, Jacob Marshal, who cut the steps. The River Noe is now flowing in a deep gorge to your left.

At the bottom of the Ladder, a packhorse bridge is met and a level track takes you to Upper Booth, just over a mile distant. From Upper Booth there is a climb of about 300 feet up to an undulating area where there has been an obvious landslip. In just over a mile from Upper Booth, the end of the Pennine Way is reached at Grindsbrook Booth.

The village of Edale should more properly be called Grindsbrook Booth but has adopted the name of the valley. For the next two miles down the valley you will have magnificent views of the ridgeway on the other side of the valley between Mam Tor and Lose Hill.

In Edale, take the path behind " The Nag's Head" across a packhorse bridge towards Ollerbrook Booth. In about half a mile from Ollerbrook Booth, there is a house set amongst some trees on the left (Woodhouse Farm). Climb the field to skirt the top edge of these trees.

In about half a mile, the Youth Hostel is reached. The path goes through the Youth Hostel grounds and follows the high ground past Clough Farm towards Jaggers Clough.

At Jaggers Clough, Hope Cross and the line of the old Roman Road from the Ashop valley to Navio are above you. Take the path to the right into the wood which descends to the River Noe at Edale End. At the river, do not take the path over the bridge, but turn left into the field and follow the river. In the woods the river descends a series of small rapids.

When the road is reached, turn left for about 100 yards, go under the railway bridge and then take the footpath down to a small holding on the right (Normans Farm). For the next mile, the path follows the river downstream, the view being dominated by Lose Hill above on the right. At Townhead Bridge take the road which goes down to Hope.

In Hope, cross the Bamford to Castleton Road and then the Peakshole Water before taking the road to the left up the hill (Eccles Lane). This leads to a path across the fields to Brough. In about a mile the path actually crosses the old Roman Fort of Navio just above the River Noe.

The junction of the River Noe with the River Derwent is now only about a mile and a half away and this is reached by taking the minor road from Brough through Shatton to the river bridge over the Noe, where the walk ends.

Hope Valley walk (Map 11.2)

From Castleton, take Goosehill Lane which climbs to the west away from the Peakshole Water. The lane passes behind Goosehill Hall and then becomes a path which skirts the base of the hill to the bottom of Winnats Pass.

Cross the road at Speedwell Cavern and join the old road towards Mam Tor. Treak Cliff Cavern is on the left and, a little further ahead, the Odin Mine is on the right. Here you can see the lead ore crushing floor with its abandoned wheel and cast iron base plate. In the summer look on the spoil heaps for the diminutive white five petalled leadwort, which is normally an indication of lead in the soil.

The Ridgeway, Mam Tor

Further along, slippage of the shale has caused spectacular distortion of the roadway. It is no wonder that Derbyshire County Council gave up the unequal struggle to mend this road in 1979. If the wind is from the east, hang gliders use the top of this road as a launching area and it is possible to watch them at close hand.

Follow the abandoned road until the A625 is reached. Turn right here and follow the main road for a short distance until the Mam Tor car park is reached. Take the path which leads up to the top of the Mam Tor.

From Mam Tor, take the ridgeway path towards Lose Hill passing Hollins Cross (an important crossing point between the Edale and Hope valleys) and Back Tor. This two-mile path between Mam Tor and Lose Hill has been an important transport route back into antiquity, and gives superb views not only over the Edale and Hope valleys but far beyond.

The descent from Lose Hill towards Hope is across open grassland until a wooded packhorse hollow-way is reached which leads to Townhead and the road to Hope.

In Hope, cross the A625, pass the church on your left and descend to the Peakshole Water. A little way up the hill a gravelled path is signposted to the right. This path follows the Peakshole Water to Castleton.

Just outside Hope the path crosses the railway line to the Cement Works and on the outskirts of Castleton there is an unusual reservoir on the other side of the river. The Peakshole Water is one of several rivers whose water may be diverted into the Derwent Reservoirs.

Places of interest in the Edale/Hope valleys

11.1 Bradwell

Much like Middleton by Wirksworth further south, there is a legend that Bradwell was a Roman slave camp serving the local lead mining industry. No one-horse town, Bradwell has, in addition to lead mining, been a centre for a diverse range of manufacturing – felt hats ("Bradder Beavers"), optical lenses, umbrellas, cement and ice cream.

The Bradwell Brook was one of the boundaries of the Royal Peak Forest. An old defensive work which climbs the hill to Rebellion Knoll, the Grey Ditch, is thought to date back to the time of enmity between Mercia and Northumbria.

Bagshawe Mine, with its 130 steps, was discovered by miners in 1806 and is named after the first proprietor.

11.2 Castleton

William Peveril built the castle above Castleton in 1076 to protect the Royal Peak Forest and the local lead mines on the site of an earlier Saxon fort. In 1157, Henry the Second and Malcolm the Fourth of Scotland met at the castle and the latter was "persuaded" to give up Cumberland, Westmorland and Northumbria.

The original entrance to the castle was not the present steep tourist path from Castleton, but rather a gentler approach along the ridge from the west and over a wooden bridge.

Castleton church is a Saxon foundation, although the earliest remaining fabric is the impressive Norman arch with its chevron moulding. The majority of the building is, however, either 17th or 19th century. The box pews and the Breeches Bible date from the 17th century.

Both castle and church belonged to the Peveril family only until 1269. One of Wiiliam's descendants forfeited his lands to the Crown, after poisoning the Earl of Chester (the husband of his mistress).

The 17th century Hall is now a Youth Hostel.

The Garland Procession on 29 May ostensibly celebrates the restoration of the Monarchy in 1660 after 11 years of Cromwell's Commonwealth, but probably has earlier origins.

The source of the Peakshole Water, a clear limestone stream, is below Peak Cavern. The entrance to Peak Cavern once housed several buildings, including an Inn. Rope manufacture was carried out in the cave from the 15th century until 1957. The public has access as far as the Great Chamber and further passages extend several miles into the hillside.

11.3 Edale

The village of Edale should more correctly be called Grindsbrook
Booth but is, by common usage, named after the valley. Throughout
its history, Edale has primarily been a dairy farming centre. This is
reflected in the collection of Booths which make up Edale – Upper,
Barber, Grindsbrook, Oller and Nether; booth being a temporary
shelter for herdsmen and cattle.

The only industrial activity in the valley was at a mill at Nether
Booth which operated from 1793 to 1934, successively as cornmill,
tannery and cotton mill. Things might have been different, for there
have been plans to form a massive reservoir which would have
flooded the valley and, just before the Second World War, to build
a steelworks. Both plans were successfully resisted.

Edale has been a major rambling centre for over a century. In 1863
it was made accessible when the Manchester to Sheffield railway
opened. In 1965, the 250 mile Pennine Way, which starts at the Nag's
Head, was inaugurated.

11.4 Hope

Hope is one of the largest parishes in the country, covering two
thirds of the Royal Peak Forest established after the Norman Conquest. The settlement of Hope predates the Normans, the church
having a cross and a font which are of the Saxon period. The church
also has two fine 13th century forester tombstones showing outlines
of forestry equipment, and a 17th century Breeches Bible.

The cement works was set up in 1928, its location taking advantage of both the primary materials required being close at hand –
limestone and shale.

There is a Well Dressing in June and a Show on the August Bank
Holiday.

11.5 Lose Hill and Win Hill

Legend has it that, after a 7th century battle between Northumbria
and Mercia, victors and vanquished camped on these hills thereby
giving them their names. Both these 1500 feet hills on opposite sides

of the River Noe give splendid views over the surrounding country-side. Losehill Hall houses the National Park Residential Centre.

11.6 Mam Tor

At 16 acres, the hill fort at Mam Tor is the largest in the Peak District, enclosing some 100 circular huts. The fort, which was established in the late Bronze Age/Early Iron Age, has its own small spring. The ancient ridgeway between Mam Tor and Lose Hill gives extensive views over both Dark and White Peak.

11.7 Navio

When the Romans built their fort at Brough in AD 158 it was probably to control the local lead mines. Built at the confluence of the River Noe and the Bradwell Brook, the fort was named after the Noe which formed a defensive feature.

Excavations early in the 20th century uncovered an underground strongroom. Although there is no evidence of this on the ground today, there are photographs of the excavation in the Sheffield Museum.

The Roman Road from Navio to Buxton is called Batham Gate – the road to the Baths. The Roman Road to Glossop is to be seen near Hope Cross.

11.8 Odin Mine

Odin is the name of a Norse god and, because of this, it is conjectured that the Danes worked the mines in the 9th and 10th centuries. Although the Romans are thought to have worked the Derbyshire lead mines and the Anglo-Saxons are definitely known to have worked the Wirksworth mines, the Odin Mine is the earliest to be recorded by name in 1280. The crusher, which is seen on the Hope valley walk, is of 1823.

In addition to lead, the mine also produced a small amount of silver (3oz per ton of lead).

11.9 Winnats Pass

There is much ·evidence for the formation of water-worn underground caverns in the Hope and Rushop valleys, and it is highly probable that the spectacular Winnats Pass was formed, at least in part, by the collapse of a cavern system.

The Pass was not always a safe place for travellers and, in 1758, a young couple on the way to their wedding at Peak Forest were set upon and murdered. (Because of its status, Peak Forest was outside the normal Church jurisdiction and, in common with Gretna Green, had more relaxed marriage requirements). Their bodies lay hidden in a cave for ten years until one of the murderers confessed his crime on his death bed. His three fellow miscreants all came to satisfactorily sticky ends.

Speedwell Mine at the bottom of Winnats Pass is an old lead mine which is open to the public. A half mile boat journey along an 18th century boat level takes the visitor to the Bottomless Pit. Water from the Speedwell Mine emerges into the Peakshole Water at Castleton.

Walk 12: River Wye

Distances:

Total: 16.8 miles

Section 1: Topley Pike to Monsal Viaduct: 6.4 miles

Section 2: Monsal Viaduct to Rowsley: 10.4 miles

Ordnance Survey map: Outdoor Leisure 24, The White Peak

Torrents of glacial meltwater cut the spectacular Wye valley into the high limestone plateau which lies between Buxton and Bakewell. The present river runs in this valley, twisting between vertical limestone cliffs sometimes three hundred feet high.

The river is naturally fast flowing, with a clean bedrock, but a succession of medieval and Industrial Revolution weirs and mills leads to a mixture of rapids and slower moving sections. Downstream, the river is famous as a trout stream, and is one of the few rivers in Britain in which rainbow trout breed.

The walk is impassable at Chee Tor during periods of flooding and, just downstream of Chee Tor gorge, some scrambling over rocks is necessary.

Although a number of the Wye's subsidiary dry valleys have been spoilt by roads, several are worth walking including Monksdale, Tideswell Dale (the lower section) and Deep Dale (south west of Monsal Dale).

Being in a limestone area, the Wye is very rewarding for anyone interested in flowers. The geology also is interesting, with volcanics intruding into the limestones and previously important lead, "marble" and chert mines.

The towns of the Wye – Buxton, Ashford, Bakewell and Tideswell – have much to interest the visitor, and Haddon Hall is one of the best preserved medieval houses in Britain.

There is parking at regular intervals down the valley.

Bakewell Bridge

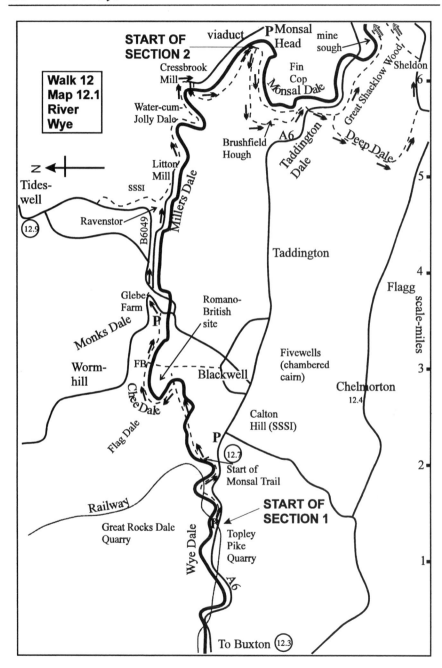

Walk 12
Map 12.1
River
Wye

START OF
SECTION 2

viaduct

PMonsal
Head

mine
sough

Sheldon

Cressbrook
Mill

Fin
Cop

Monsal Dale

Great Shacklow Wood

6

Water-cum-
Jolly Dale

Brushfield
Hough

A6

Taddington
Dale

Deep Dale

N

Tides-
well

Litton
Mill

SSSI

Millers Dale

5

Ravenstor

B6049

Taddington

4

Flagg

scale-miles

Glebe
Farm

Romano-
British
site

Monks Dale

P

Fivewells
(chambered
cairn)

Chelmorton

12.4

3

Worm-
hill

FB

Chee Dale

Blackwell

Flag Dale

Calton
Hill (SSSI)

P

12.7

Start of
Monsal Trail

2

Railway

Great Rocks Dale
Quarry

Wye Dale

P

Topley
Pike
Quarry

START OF
SECTION 1

A6

1

To Buxton 12.3

12.9

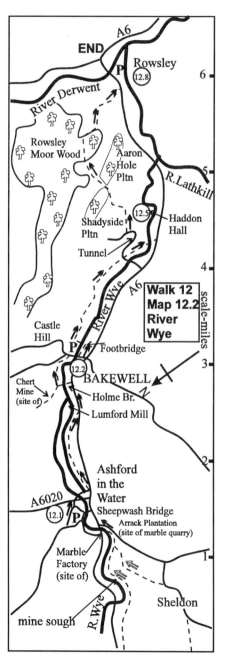

The Walk

Section 1: Topley Pike to Monsal Viaduct

Distance: 6.4 miles

Starting point: SK103725

Map: 12.1

Considering the beauty of the valley to be seen later, the first few miles east of Buxton are, to say the least, unpromising. Road, railway and sewerage works jostle to fill the narrow valley bottom.

Things start to look up however as Topley Pike is approached. The car park opposite the Topley Pike Quarry is the first access point to the Monsal Trail. (There is another car park which also gives access to the Trail about half a mile along the road at the top of Topley Pike).

From the first car park, take the track along the river bank. To your left, there is open hillside. To your right there is a wood with shade loving plants such as the Cuckoo Pint. You pass twice under the railway line which carries the limestone out of the quarries in Great Rocks Dale.

Some half a mile after leaving the car park, the railway divides into two lines; one curving north into Great Rocks Dale while the other proceeds ahead. The line down the valley was closed in 1968 and has now been converted into a footpath (the Monsal Trail). There are some steps up the railway embankment to access the Trail.

There has been a mill and a river crossing in the valley below the start of the Trail since medieval times. Before the building of the turnpike down the valley in 1810, the roads ran across rather than down the valley. To the right, a track may be seen coming down the small valley from Topley Pike. This was one of the medieval routes between Derby and Manchester.

For the next mile, proceed down the railway track which crosses the river twice and twice goes through short tunnels. Enormous quantities of material were used to embank the line and the railway represents a feat of Victorian engineering.

On crossing the second bridge, the track goes into Chee Tor tunnel (which is closed). Chee Tor must be harder than the rock previously traversed, for at this point the river is turned back on itself and for a short distance runs westwards.

Take the path down to the river, cross the footbridge and then follow the path under the railway bridge. Some stepping stones are reached which are not passable when the river is in flood.

The cliffs on both sides of the river tower hundreds of feet above, and it is difficult to visualise just what flow of water was needed to carve through this hard material. Notice the rockface on the left, where the cliff has been considerably undercut. The path ahead to Flag Dale requires a scramble up from the river over a couple of rocky promontories.

Shortly after passing a small stream coming down from Flag Dale the valley widens and the river descends over a series of weirs to a footbridge. This leads to a path which climbs over Chee Tor to Blackwell.

If time allows, it is well worth the few minutes to climb this hill. From the top of the hill there is are good views looking down on the serpentine gorge at Chee Tor. At this point, the railway is in the tunnel directly beneath. In the field to the right of the path you can see evidence of earthworks. This was a Romano-British site. Pottery finds have dated it to the 3rd and 4th centuries AD.

Take the path back down to the river. A short distance downstream, some steps are reached which take you back up to the railway track which has just emerged from the tunnel. Towards the top of the flight of steps are some good crinoidal fossils.

In about half a mile, the large car park at Miller's Dale station is reached. Information boards show some of the many flowers to be seen in the vicinity including

- ¤ Globe Flower (May-June)
- ¤ Meadow Saxifrage (April-May)
- ¤ Common Orchid (June-Aug)
- ¤ Leadwort (May-Aug)
- ¤ Jacob's Ladder (June-July)
- ¤ Cowslips (March-May)
- ¤ Ox Eye Daisy (May-Sept)
- ¤ Dark Mullein (June-Oct)

After the station, the Monsal Trail crosses one of the bridges and follows the track to Litton Mill just over a mile away. The problem with this section of the Trail is that the trees are beginning to become rather overgrown, considerably reducing the opportunities to see the valley below.

A more interesting alternative is to walk along the valley bottom road. Leave the station car park, turn left up the hill and, when Glebe Farm is reached (on the corner), take the track down the hill to the river. Cross the B6049 and take the minor road directly ahead which passes the Anglers Rest towards Litton Mill. Whilst this is a road without a footpath, it is a cul-de-sac, and is normally fairly quiet.

Again, the river is bounded by high limestone cliffs and the slopes down to the road are rich in flowers. In the early summer, look out for the delicate white Nottingham Catchfly and the lovely deep colouration of the Bloody Cranesbill. Also look out for the point on the left-hand side immediately adjacent to the road where a long strip of volcanic lava outcrops. (The Peak District was volcanically active at the time when the limestone was being deposited, and volcanic material was injected into many of the limestone bedding planes).

After passing the Youth Hostel at Ravenstor, there is a path to the left to Tideswell. It is well worth the detour up the dry valley to Tideswell.

Part way up the dry valley, there is an old quarry of some geological interest, which has been designated a Site of Special Scientific Interest. Volcanic rock was mined here, and the old quarry has now been converted into an attractive picnic area.

In a little under half a mile from the bottom of Tideswell Dale, Litton Mill is reached. This mill had a very unsavoury reputation for cruelty towards its child labour force.

The path goes through the grounds of the mill before proceeding down the rather unusually named Water-cum-Jolly Dale to Cressbrook Mill.

Cressbrook Mill, originally owned by Arkwright, has had a varied history, including the rather unlikely manufacture of peppermint. The site is now used for stone processing, and the mill building is in a state of some dilapidation.

Take the path over the weir to the other side of the river, and then climb up and across the hillside. From this path there are good views down the valley toward Monsal Head. The path reaches the Monsal Head viaduct in just under a mile.

The building of this bridge much upset John Ruskin, and it drew from him the bitter comment "– now every fool in Buxton can be at Bakewell in half and hour, and every fool in Bakewell at Buxton".

Section 2: Monsal Viaduct to Rowsley

Distance: 10.4 miles

Starting point: SK183715

Map: 12.2

Although you will be going down the west side of Monsal Dale, do go onto the viaduct to see the views which are justly famous. From the viaduct there is a choice of two paths down the valley to Taddington Dale.

The first path is over the meadowlands at the river's edge and is accessed from the western end of the viaduct.

The second path starts from the same place, but climbs steeply up the hill from the Viaduct to the top of the hill. It then traverses the top of the hill for about a mile before bearing left, following a sign to Brushfield Hough. After passing behind Brushfield Hough, the path reaches a promontory high above Taddington Dale. From the promontory, the path descends through the woodland to join the valley bottom path as it proceeds to the A6.

Monsal Dale is not only attractive, but it is also accessible to the motorist. At peak periods it can be very crowded. Because of the steep climb, fewer people use the high level route. This route also has the benefit of splendid views down onto the river and over to Fin Cop on the other side of the valley.

When the A6 is reached, cross the road and go through the car park. Take the path ahead which climbs towards Deep Dale. Here there is a choice between Deep Dale and Great Shacklow Wood.

The most direct path is through the wood, which is one of the premier ash woods in the country. The wood itself is attractive and is sufficiently open to support birds. When the river is reached, look out for a fairly large flow of water coming into the river. This is not a stream but is a "sough" bringing water from the Magpie Mine a mile away. Shortly after the sough, there is a water mill which was used to cut bobbins for the Nottingham textile industry and also to pump water to the mining village of Sheldon above.

The alternative to the Great Shacklow Wood route is to take the path up Deep Dale. The attraction of this valley is the profusion of flowers in early summer, including Early Purple Orchids, Cowslips and Meadow Saxifrage.

Towards the top of Deep Dale, a path leads over the brow of the hill towards Sheldon. (To the South may be seen the derelict Magpie Lead Mine). Just before leaving Sheldon, take the path across the fields towards Ashford. Here you may see a carpet of yellow mountain pansies. When the path divides, take the right fork.

Just after the river is reached, the site of the old Ashford Marble Factory is seen ahead. Follow the minor road which, in a short distance, meets the A6. A little way down the A6 you come to the very attractive and photogenic Sheepwash Bridge. There has been a river crossing here going back to Iron Age times.

Mine sough below Great Shacklow Wood

From Sheepwash Bridge it is often possible to see substantial rainbow trout. The Wye is one of the few rivers in the country where the rainbow trout breed naturally (elsewhere they are stocked). It is thought that the breeding in the Wye is associated with the water temperature. To hatch, the ova of the rainbow trout require higher temperatures than our native brown trout. The Wye is fed by a number of warm springs, and these keep the river above the critical temperature. Cross Sheepwash Bridge and turn down the road to the right. The church, on the left, has an unusual Norman tympanum over the door, which features strange beasts.

Crossing the A6020 you shortly come to two bridges. The inscription on the first reads M. HYDE 1664, recording the unfortunate man who was blown from his horse and drowned in the river.

Rejoin the A6 for a few yards and take the path across the fields towards Bakewell. You are now leaving the limestone country, with its gorge like scenery. The landscape for the rest of the river is gentler and more undulating. The one and a half miles to Bakewell is attractive countryside with small hillocks and the river below.

Coming out of the fields it is necessary to walk a short distance alongside the A6. Pass the Lumford Mill (once an Arkwright Mill), before coming to a most attractive packhorse bridge. Cross the bridge, take the road to the right and then the path across the river meadows to the main Bakewell bridge. The oldest part of the bridge is of the 13th century and may be seen on the downstream side.

From the bridge follow the path downstream on the west bank to a footbridge. Cross this, and the adjacent field, to come to the mill leat. After the leat, turn right into the Bakewell Showground. The path ahead crosses the meadows, occasionally touching the river which is sinuous, clear and fast-flowing.

Just over a mile from Bakewell the path divides. If you intend to visit Haddon Hall, take the right fork which crosses the river. If not, take the left fork to Rowsley, starting a climb of some 300 feet.

Initially a farm track is followed which crosses the old London to Manchester railway line at the point where it enters a tunnel under the Haddon estate. Shortly after passing the tunnel entry, a path bears right leaving the farm track and climbing up to Bowling Green Farm.

Behind the farm you will come to a point where two plantations meet (Shadyside and Aaron Hole). Ignore the sign here marked Rowsley (to the right) and proceed behind Aaron Hole plantation. To your left there is a splendid view down a long narrow valley back to Bakewell.

The path ahead touches the tip of a wood on the left (a path to Chatsworth enters the wood here) and shortly afterwards crosses the corner of Rowsley Moor Wood. Emerging from the wood the path bears right and descends to Rowsley where the Wye flows into the Derwent.

Places of interest in the Wye valley

12.1 Ashford in the Water

This is an attractive village set on the river, and it must have been considerably improved by the A6 bypass. Ashford was on the old Portway and there has been an important crossing of the Wye here going back into prehistoric times. In the medieval period it was an important packhorse centre.

The 17th century Sheepwash Bridge incorporates a sheepfold and is one of the major attractions of the village. A bridge further down the river bears the inscription "M. Hyde, 1664". This records the misfortune of a man blown from his horse in a gale and drowned in the river.

Holy Trinity Church has a Norman Tympanium over the door depicting wild animals. Inside there are paper garlands which were carried at the funerals of unmarried girls and also examples of work in "Ashford Marble".

"Ashford Marble" is not actually a marble, but rather a fine grained bituminous limestone which takes a high polish. It was mined at a number of quarries in the locality, including one in the Arrack plantation, and was worked in the factory, at the west end of the village, which was cut in two by the building of the A6 bypass.

The six wells are "dressed" in May or June.

12.2 Bakewell

While most of the buildings in Bakewell are of the 19th century, Bakewell has probably been continuously settled back into the Iron Age. Points of interest include:

¤ an Iron Age fort looking down on the town above the golf course (Ball Cross)

¤ the probable site of a bath at the warm spring in Roman times (a Roman altar found nearby is to be seen at Haddon Hall)

¤ the Anglo-Saxon Chronicle tells that King Edward visited Bakewell in AD924 when recovering the Peak District from the Danes and ordered the building of a fort (exact site unknown)

¤ in the Domesday Survey, Bakewell had two priests. This indicated a centre of some importance.

¤ Two fine bridges over the Wye; the main bridge dates back to 1300 and Holme Bridge (packhorse bridge) to 1664.

Just up the path from Holme Bridge there are extensive mineworkings in the hillside where chert was extracted. The chert was transported to Cheddleton (see Churnet valley walk) were it was processed in a watermill for use in the Staffordshire pottery industry.

The church has a noted Anglo-Saxon cross and probably the finest collection of medieval carved gravestones in Britain. These were found during renovation work in 1841/2, and are now in the church porch.

In common with Buxton and Matlock, Bakewell has a warm water spring. The first Duke of Rutland tried to develop the town as a spa, by building a bathhouse in 1697. Probably because the temperature of the spring was lower than those at Buxton and Matlock, the venture at Bakewell was never a success. The Duke's 33 by 11 foot bath still exists, although it is not open to the public.

Perhaps Bakewell's greatest success also sprang from a failure. In 1860 a cook put the ingredients for a pudding into her dish in the wrong order. In doing she created the Bakewell Pudding.

12.3 Buxton

The curative properties of Buxton's hot spring waters has been its main attraction to outsiders throughout the ages. Also of interest:

¤ the Romans had a settlement here throughout their occupation of Britain which they called *Aquae Arnemetiae*

¤ Mary Queen of Scots came for relief of her rheumatism when she was a prisoner of the Earl of Shrewsbury at Chatsworth

¤ the Fifth Duke of Devonshire commissioned John Carr to build the Crescent (1780-90), centring the development around the thermal waters. It is said that the Duke financed the Crescent from the profit of his copper mine at Ecton (see Manifold valley walk).

Behind the Crescent is the Opera House. The Buxton festival is held there in July. The old Pump Room is now the Buxton Micrarium. The Buxton Museum has an excellent display of archeology of the Peak District.

12.4 Chelmorton

This is a linear village set below its water supply (the Illy Willy Water). The village has probably the best preserved set of medieval strip fields in the country, its long narrow fields being set at right angles to the road.

Just to the east of the village is the 5000 year old Five Wells Chambered Cairn (not on a public path). Excavated in 1846, the tomb yielded 12 skeletons. There is a replica of the site in the Buxton Museum.

12.5 Haddon Hall

Haddon Hall is claimed to be the best example of a non-fortified medieval house in Britain.

At one time, Haddon was the principal residence of the Duke of Rutland but, when the family seat was moved to Belvoir Castle in the late 17th century, the Hall was left virtually unused for almost 200 years. Haddon's uniqueness springs from this period of benign neglect.

The oldest part of the Hall dates back to 1080-90, when it was part of the estate of William Peveril. The Banqueting Hall is of around 1350.

Apart from the fabric of the building, Haddon is perhaps best-known for the story of the elopement of Dorothy Vernon with John Manners. The story, later immortalised by Sir Walter Scott, does not appear to have been tarnished by the realisation that the steps down which Dorothy is supposed to have eloped were not built until 26 years after her marriage.

12.6 Magpie Mine

This mine near Sheldon contains the most complete lead mining remains in the Peak District.

As with so many other lead mines, its future was threatened when the water table was reached. A Cornish Beam Engine was installed in 1868, but the cost of fuelling the engine was so high that a sough was built as a cheaper alternative (1873-81). The sough discharges into the Wye below the Great Shacklow Wood.

The mine continued to operate until 1920 and, for a spell, in the 1950s. Lack of maintenance following the mine closure caused a partial collapse of the sough and, in 1962, water backed up and emerged in Shacklow Wood, causing a 30 foot crater. The sough discharge is seen on the Wye walk at SK179696 and is just visible from the A6.

12.7 Monsal Trail

In 1849 the Midland Railway reached Rowsley on its intended route to Manchester. Problems then arose for the railway company when both the Dukes of Devonshire and of Rutland refused to have the railway pass through their estates.

Matters were resolved when the Duke of Rutland allowed the railway to pass under the Haddon Estate and, after a considerable feat of engineering, the line reached Buxton in 1863.

From the junction in Miller's Dale, a second line was built through Great Rocks Dale to reach Manchester in 1863. The line operated for about a century and was closed in 1968 (except for the line up Great

Rocks Dale which takes limestone out of the quarry towards Buxton). A nine mile section between Great Rocks Dale and Bakewell has been converted into a walk – the Monsal Trail. Because of the high expense of upkeep of the tunnels, most have been blocked off and require a detour.

12.8 Rowsley

(See Derwent Valley walk)

12.9 Tideswell

This attractive village is best-known for its magnificent 14th century church ("the Cathedral of the Peak"), and its fine main street with a coaching inn of 1730 (The George Inn). The building of the church was interrupted by the plague of 1349/50 and took 75 years to complete.

In the early medieval period, Tideswell was an important royal centre, being on the southern edge of the Royal Peak Forest. It was visited by Edward the First, Edward the Third and Henry the Fourth.

Two of its residents played important roles in the turbulent 16th century. The astute and powerful Bishop Pursglove died enormously wealthy as a result of helping Henry the Eighth to dissolve the Monasteries. He survived and prospered by changing his religious allegiance three times under different monarchs, but was finally forced into retirement when he felt unable to change a fourth time.

School teacher Nicholas Garlick was not so fortunate. Trained as a Catholic priest on the continent, Garlick was found in hiding with another priest at Padley (see Derwent valley walk) and was hung, drawn and quartered at Derby.

The subtle difference between the two men, which allowed one Catholic priest to prosper and another to be killed, is that Bishop Purglove was ordained in England whereas Garlick had actively sought ordination on the continent after it had been made illegal in England. Pursglove was regarded as merely misguided, whereas Garlick was suspected of being sympathetic to a foreign power (at a time when Spain was threatening to invade the country to restore a Catholic monarchy).

Social and Economic Development

At the end of the Ice Age, Britain was still connected to the continent and the first Old Stone Age hunters crossed the continental land-bridge following herds of reindeer, mammoths and whooly rhino. They left evidence of their visits in the flints and animal bone remains found in the caves of the Manifold, Dove and Lathkill.

The Middle Stone Age from about 5000BC was still a period of nomadic hunting, but there is some evidence of the use of fire for forest clearing. Tools were improving and extensive use was made of local Derbyshire Chert, a material which would find use several millennia later in the Staffordshire pottery industry.

The first farmers came to the Peak District in about 3000BC, considerably later than in lowland Britain. These New Stone Age people were still users of stone implements, now fine grained axes from Langdale in the Lake District rather than flints.

No longer was this subsistence living, for they built some dozen megalithic monuments which required a considerable investment of labour. Arbor Low, which is the third largest megalithic monu-ment in Britain after Stonehenge and Avebury, is estimated to have involved a million man hours in its construction.

Bronze Age or Beaker People, named after their highly decorated vessels, inhabited the Peak District from about 2000BC. There are important Bronze Age sites in the Derwent valley.

The most striking remains of the Iron Age period (700BC to the Roman Invasion) are to be seen in their dozen hill forts, the most impressive being Mam Tor which is included in the Hope Valley walk. The enigma of these people is that apart from their forts they left so few artefacts.

The Romans occupied the Peak District between approximately AD70 and AD400. Unlike the south of England which was civilian,

Northern England was under military control; the purpose of the occupation being to secure the northern border.

The Roman army in Britain comprised three Legions (York, Chester and Caerleon) and three to four dozen Auxilia. The Legions, which were 5000-6000 strong, were Roman Citizens and were based in fortresses of about 50 acres. Apart from their Roman officers, the Auxilia were conscripts who only became Roman citizens on their eventual discharge. About 500 strong, the Auxilia were housed in forts of two to eight acres. The known Roman sites in the Peak District were Auxilia forts at Brough (Navio), Glossop (Melandra) and Rocester, although there are also a number of other small forts which it has been suggested are Roman. Navio is included in the River Noe walk and there is a good display of the excavation of the site at the Sheffield Museum.

In the White Peak, some 40 Romano-British sites have been discovered. The thermal waters (81°F) at Buxton attracted the Romans to establish baths there and remains were uncovered when the Crescent was built.

Following the Roman withdrawal from Britain in AD408, there is little direct evidence of developments in the Peak District until the Domesday Survey of 1086. What evidence we have is inferential.

The Angles and Saxons settled southern and eastern England, and from analysis of place names and the Anglo-Saxon cemeteries it would seem it was some two hundred years before their presence was felt in the Peak District. Our picture of life in 5th and 6th century England is one of small kingdoms fighting each other for territorial dominance. Certainly, there are many legends of battles on Peak District soil; perhaps the best-known being the battle in the Hope valley in which the victors and vanquished afterwards camped on Win Hill and Lose Hill respectively.

By the 7th century, however, these small kingdoms had coalesced and England was in effect controlled by three kingdoms – Northumbria, Mercia and Wessex – the Peak District being part of Mercian territory controlled from the royal centre at Repton.

Stability brought with it an increasing prosperity, but also a reduced attention to defence. From about AD800, England started to attract Scandinavian interest in the form of almost annual raids.

By AD873 the Danish Army had subjugated Mercia. Overwintering their Army that year at the sacked Mercian royal centre of Repton they decided to split the Army:

¤ the northern Army under Halfdane was to settle Northumbria

¤ the southern Army under Guthrun was to lead the onslaught on Wessex.

The latter's objective was almost achieved with Wessex control under Alfred being reduced to a small area in the Somerset marshes. However, in a remarkable reverse, Alfred defeated Guthrun and forced him to accept the Treaty of Wedmore (AD886). Under this treaty, the Danes were to confine their influence to an area to the north and east of a line which ran roughly from London to Chester.

The Peak District was therefore firmly under Danelaw, with York being the capital and Derby the local administrative centre. This position however was to be relatively short-lived, for the English then started a slow campaign of attrition to recapture the land under Danish control, capturing Chester (AD907), Stafford/Tamworth (AD913), Derby (AD917), Thelwell/Manchester (AD920), Bakewell (AD920) and York (AD954).

Although the main Danish settlement areas were to the north in Yorkshire and Cumbria, there is considerable circumstantial evidence of colonisation in the Peak District:

¤ From place names: there is a line of settlements stretching from Cheshire towards Derby with names of Norse origin such as Thornsett, Kettleshulme, Hulme End and Thorpe.

¤ From crosses: those at Eyam (Derwent walk) and Bakewell (Wye walk) include Norse motifs.

¤ A treasure hoard found in a cave at Beeston Tor (Manifold walk) and now in the British museum can be dated from its coins to around AD875. Throughout Northern England, there is a strong correlation between Anglo-Saxon hidden treasure and Danish raids. There are a large number of finds dating from the AD870s but an almost total absence from the subsequent period of peace. It can be no coincidence that the treasure hoard is directly on the line of place names with Norse names, the inference being that Norse colonists from Ireland travelled up the Mersey and through the Goyt and Manifold valleys.

For a period after their expulsion from England, the Danes concentrated their attention elsewhere, but from about AD990 they started raiding England again, extorting vast tributes in the form of Danegeld. Indeed, these tributes became so onerous that England eventually fell directly under the control of the Danish King. This control however was unstable, particularly on the death of a king.

When Edward the Confessor died, there was a three-cornered fight between the English Harold, Tostig the Dane and William the Norman. Although William prevailed, the Danes represented a serious threat, particularly in alliance with the former Danelaw. William was ruthless in neutralising the threat and laid waste vast tracts of the north which were recorded in the Domesday Survey as "wasta est".

The earliest extant buildings in the Peak District are from the Norman period, there being no remains from the previous Anglo-Saxon and Danish periods. This might be thought surprising, since Mercia had become Christian in the 7th century and had established churches throughout the region from that period. These early churches had however been of wooden construction and none has survived. Only at the royal centre at Repton, which is outside the Peak District, is there a crypt of the Anglo-Saxon period which still exists.

Even most of the early Norman stone architecture has not survived later rebuilding programmes, and there are only two churches which are relatively original – Steetley and Melbourne. Neither of these is included in any of the walks, but Norman elements may be seen in several churches including Thorpe (River Dove), Ashford in the Water (River Wye) and Youlgreave (River Lathkill/Bradford). Peveril Castle and Haddon Hall also contains elements from the Norman period.

What has survived of the Anglo-Saxon and Danish periods is an abundance of artefacts – stone crosses and fonts, to be seen in many churches and church yards. The best preserved cross is at Eyam and a particularly fine piece of Anglo-Saxon carving is to be seen in the church at Wirksworth, its state of preservation owing much to the fact that it had been buried under the floor for several centuries. It is of some concern that so many of these early examples of Peak District heritage are languishing in the open, where they are being attacked by the elements. It must surely be possible to relocate the best of these works indoors. There, they might be both better preserved and more imaginatively displayed.

The earliest population estimate for the Peak District exists in a Mercian document of the 7th century called the Tribal Hidage. This suggests that there were about 1200 families living in Pecsaetan. This is also the earliest written record of the word from which "Peak" has been derived.

Although there must be some reservations about its detailed accuracy, the Domesday Survey suggests that the total population of Staffordshire and Derbyshire at the time was about 6000, with each settlement having an average population of about 30 mainly agricultural workers. The major landowners of this feudal society were the King, a small number of his Barons, and the Heads of Monastic Houses.

To the north of the region was an area almost devoid of habitation and this was probably the result of the Norman military campaign to subjugate the north. For some five hundred years, the 200 square miles roughly bounded by the rivers Goyt, Etherow, Derwent, Bradwell Brook and Wye were held by the Crown as the Royal Forest and reserved for hunting by the King.

From the time of the conversion of Mercia to Christianity in AD653 to the Dissolution of the Monasteries in 1538, the Church accumulated progressively more land in the Peak District. In addition to the ecclesiastical foundations themselves, (for example, Dieulacresse and Croxden), large areas of land were given as endowments to distant ecclesiastical foundations. Over 40 granges are known to have belonged to monastic orders and most of the farms with grange in their title have an ecclesiastical origin. Nor were the endowments only land, with many other forms of economic enterprise such as forges and mines belonging to the church (lead mining at Wirksworth was owned by Repton Abbey).

Whilst no reliable records exist which allow measurement of the economic growth during the medieval period, the erection of new buildings is always a useful barometer of an economy. Building requires a long term perspective, and is rarely undertaken unless there is a degree of optimism about the future.

During the period known as the "Age of Faith" (the 11th to the 15th centuries) most of the building was done by the Church. We have already seen that the Norman period was a period of considerable church building and similarly the 13th and 14th centuries also saw many fine churches either built or considerably extended, including Ashbourne, Bakewell and Tideswell.

In contrast, for the two centuries following the plague of 1348-50, no significant church buildings were erected in the Peak District. During this period, many churches in more prosperous regions were being built in the Perpendicular style. Absence of this style from the Peak District suggests a period of poverty and stagnation. (Tideswell is interesting in that it was started just before the plague but then took 75 years to complete).

The 16th century was also a period of some upheaval in the Peak District with:

¤ large estates previously held by the Church passing into other hands

¤ religious tensions heightened by the threat of a Spanish Invasion. Many of the major families in the Peak District had remained Catholic and their allegiance to a Protestant Crown was seen as suspect

¤ the imprisonment in the area, and subsequent execution, of the Catholic Mary Queen of Scots who must have created a focus for dissent.

It was not until the 17th century that we see a general resurgence of affluence and confidence. This was reflected in a large increase in the amount of building being undertaken. Not this time for the Church, but rather Halls for the gentry. Halls from this period are to be seen on most of the walks.

The 18th century saw a population explosion in England. The expanding cities, particularly of the East Midlands, caused an increase in the demand not only for Peak District agricultural products but also for animals and goods which had to be transported to these new markets. Part of the drove road between Congleton and Nottingham is incorporated into the beginning of the Churnet valley walk.

At the beginning of the 18th century, transport across the Peak District was primarily by packhorse, whether the goods being transported were wool, copper ore, coal, salt (from the Cheshire saltmines) or malt (being carried on the return journey). When Bonnie Prince Charlie crossed the rivers Dane, Churnet, Dove and Derwent on his abortive attempt to seize the crown in 1745, the roads he travelled would have changed little since early medieval times. As the industrial economy began to gather pace, this transport system became totally inadequate for the volume of goods being transported. The century between 1730 and 1830 saw a total transformation in the transport system with the establishment of:

¤ a comprehensive system of turnpike roads

¤ three canals of economic importance to the region

¤ the first railway (the Cromford and High Peak Railway of 1830).

Although the railways and canals have long ceased to have an industrial economic value, they are now a considerable leisure amenity. Several have been converted to pathways and cycle tracks. Since grazing animals are also in general excluded, many of these "linear parks" have become areas of rich flora.

In addition to agriculture, the other main economic activities in the Peak District have been mining and textiles. Lead mining was carried out in the Peak District back in Roman times (it is thought that ingots with the inscription LUTUDARUM came from a Roman mine in the Wirksworth area) and the Domesday Book records the smelting of lead at Ashford, Bakewell and Wirksworth. It is estimated that there may be as many as 50,000 abandoned mine shafts.

As the mines were progressively deepened, the lead was worked out down to the level of the water table and their viability was threatened. The volumes of water were, in general, too large to be pumped out, and the only way to dewater them was to drive "soughs" to the river valleys, sometimes several miles away. Cromford sough, built in 1688, cost £30 000 to construct, a considerable sum at that time. As we shall see later, these soughs assumed a secondary value as sources of water power when cotton production was industrialised. The lead industry was at its peak in 1700-1750 and then gradually went into decline, lead mining finally ceasing with the closure of the Mill Close mine in 1938.

Copper production in the North West has a very long history. Recently it has been shown that the copper mines at Alderley Edge in Cheshire, which had been thought to go back to Roman times, were worked during the Bronze Age. Peak District copper mining was only however to become of economic importance to the region in the late medieval period when the Duke of Devonshire found major deposits at his Ecton mine on the Manifold in the 1760s. Unlike the lead mines, the Ecton mine was almost devoid of water and by the end of the 18th century had been worked to a depth of 1400 feet, 700 feet below the level of the adjacent river Manifold. At its peak, the Ecton mine produced 4000 tons a year of copper, much of it for sheathing ships (hence copper bottomed). The ore was taken by packhorse to the Churnet valley for smelting and further processing. An industry which has evolved from this 18th century copper processing is still operational on the Churnet.

Limestone has been processed in small quantities for local farm use from the 15th century, but in 1769 the Trent and Mersey Canal Company bought the rights to Caldon Low, a limestone area between the Hamps and the Churnet. The Company commissioned the Derbyshire canal engineer James Brindley to survey a canal from the Trent and Mersey to Froghall, where they installed massive processing capacity. The limestone was transported down from Caldon Low to Froghall on one of the country's earliest tramways. The processed limestone which was transported out of Froghall by canal was used for agricultural manure, for ironmaking and for the chemical industry. It was the termination of a major contract by Brunner Mond (later to become ICI) which closed the tramway and the Froghall processing in 1920. Much interesting industrial archeology of the limestone and copper working is to be seen around the Froghall canal basin (seen on the Churnet walk).

Limestone processing is still of major importance to the economy of the Peak District. The first industrial-scale production of cotton in the world was established by Arkwright at Cromford in 1771. Arkwright came to Cromford partly to escape from the strong and sometimes violent opposition to mechanised production in existing cotton production areas and partly because of the availability of water power. Although close to the River Derwent, the water which powered the Cromford Mill was not as is often stated from the river but from the lead mine sough.

By the end of the 18th century, some 30 cotton mills had been established in Derbyshire, but this dominance was to be shortlived. By 1790, Arkwright had already established steam as a power source for cotton production and, thereafter, Lancashire with its proximity to coal established itself as the centre of cotton production.

Today, tourism is of major importance to the Peak District, attracting over 20 million visitors a year. Visitors have however been coming to see the sights since the 16th century, and several natural curiosities are marked on Saxton's first map of the Peak District of 1577.

In 1678, the political philosopher, Thomas Hobbes, who was at the time tutor at Chatsworth, published his *Wonders of the Peak*. This was essentially the first guide book to the Peak District. Hobbes' Wonders were:

¤ Chatsworth

¤ Mam Tor

¤ Eldon Hole

¤ Buxton Wells

¤ Poole's Hole

¤ Devil's Arse (Castleton)

and it is interesting to note how many of these are still major tourist attractions. *Wonders of the Peak* was co-authored by Charles Cotton of Beresford Hall. Cotton's position as Squire is reflected in the different treatment of the authors on the title page which reads

"The Latin written by Thomas Hobbes
The English by a Person of Quality".

Cotton was a man of many parts and was also co-author with Izaac Walton of the even more famous publication, *The Compleat Angler*, said to be the most famous book people have never read. Cotton's contribution to the book was the section on fly fishing.

Copies of Saxton's map and of Hobbes' Wonders of the Peak may be seen in Buxton Museum together with a Bowen map of 1767 which includes a description of each of the Wonders.

Plants in the Peak District

The Peak District has both uplands (gritstone and limestone) and deeply incised valleys. As a result, it provides a range of habitats and microclimates which support a wide variety of flora, including some nationally rare plants such as the Jacob's Ladder and pink Mezeron.

A number of plants resident in the Peak district would not normally be found in the same region. Thus, the Cloudberry and the Crowberry found at the top of the Derwent are at their southern limit in Britain while, not far away, the sunny south facing slopes of the Lathkill support the Nettle-leaved Bellflower. This Bellflower is normally associated with the south of England and is at its northern limit in the Peak District.

The plants to be found in a particular location are largely determined by the under lying rocks and the physical habitat. The table at the end of this section is a simplified summary of the plant species you might expect to find on the walks.

Often the most plant rich areas are those which are marginal from an economic point of view such as:

¤ rocky inaccessible hillsides

¤ redundant railway lines

¤ river banks which are difficult for access. (The only two places where the author has found the beautiful maroon-coloured Dusky Cranesbill have been under bushes on the river bank, one next to a sewerage works!)

The ground cover we see today in the Peak District is very different from that which would occur naturally without Man's intervention. It is possible for us to know what the earlier plant populations have been right back to the last Ice Age because of a remarkable property of Sphagnum.

Plants, when they die, are normally attacked by bacteria and fungi which recycle their constituent chemicals. Sphagnum however, when it dies and transforms to peat, creates an antibiotic. This antibiotic not only keeps the peat formed from further decay but also ensures that any pollen blown into and trapped by the peat is preserved for later analysis. The peat bogs therefore act as "time capsules", telling us much about the changing ground cover over the ages.

It would seem that a tundra type flora at the end of the Ice Age gave way first to a complete forest cover but that the forests were then progressively cleared by Man. (Today, only about 5% of the Peak District is wooded, compared with a national average of 8%).

There was an acceleration in the formation of peat on the gritstone hilltops following a climatic deterioration during the first millennium BC. This peat accumulation has been responsible for the preservation of a number of prehistoric sites, particularly in the Derwent and Etherow valleys. As the land fell out of productive use, it remained waste until the present time, thus preserving the archeological remains.

When walking on the hill-tops which have not been in agricultural use, it is always worth keeping an eye open for prehistoric artefacts. The author has a beautiful flint scraper some 5000 years old found near the summit of Win Hill on the Derwent valley walk.

Lead mining has been an important economic activity in the Peak District for perhaps 2000 years, with an estimated 50,000 disused mines. Evidence of the former mining activities may be seen in the local flora in a number of places.

Heavy metals in the soil are normally highly deleterious to both animals and plants. In many limestone areas, long strips of woodlands are to be seen in old lead mine veins, generally running in an east – west direction. These were deliberately planted to keep cattle from grazing amongst the lead workings and poisoning themselves (an example is to be seen on the Lathkill Dale walk at Long Rake just to the west of Youlgreave).

There are a few plants however which are able to tolerate heavy metals and, because of the reduction in competition from other plants which are not so tolerant, thrive on old mine workings. The

Leadwort and the Mountain Pansy are both plants which are lead tolerant. The Leadwort, a diminutive white five petalled flower, is a local name for the Spring Sandwort. It was used in former times by lead prospectors as an indication of possible ore bodies below the surface.

Grazing plays a very important role in the maintenance of a diverse flora. Land which is ungrazed will quickly revert to forest cover of Oak and Birch on sandstone and Ash on limestone. Victorian photographs of Dovedale show much less wooded hillsides than we see today, a reduction in grazing this century allowing hawthorn and subsequently ash to colonise the slopes.

Location/rock type	Gritstone/shale	Limestone
High plateau	– very acidic	– alkaline
	– accumulation of peat	– broad loamy soil
	– heather, cotton grass	traditionally, flower-rich permanent pasture supported flowers such as the Meadow Saxifrage. Modern agriculture has greatly reduced this diversity.
Slopes below plateau	– acidic	– usually alkaline (acid where soil leached)
	– restricted vegetation, e.g. bilberry, bracken, tormentil	– rocky outcrops. Rich in specialist flora such as lichen, mosses, ferns, stonecrop, herb robert.
Valley bottom	-slightly acidic	– alkaline
	– well-drained areas good for agriculture and therefore little diversity of non-economic plants	– grazed by sheep
		– herb-rich where undisturbed (e.g. Cowslips, Early Purple Orchids seen on the Wye and Dove walks).
	– boggy areas, sphagnum, rushes	

Summary of the effect of habitat on the plant distribution in the Peak District.

In a number of areas, the various conservancy bodies are encouraging either more or less grazing in order to preserve a variety of diverse habitats:

¤ at the head of the Derwent and in Padley Gorge, areas have been fenced off to encourage the regeneration of oak woodlands

¤ at The Ranger in Dimmingsdale (Churnet walk) grazing of ancient hilltop pasture is being encouraged to suppress re-afforestation and preserve the smaller plants

¤ in Lathkill Dale selective grazing is being encouraged to keep down the hawthorn and retain the extremely rich flora which in some places exceeds 50 species per square metre. (Part of Lathkill Dale has been declared a National Nature Reserve and it is a good place to see plants such as the Jabob's Ladder, cowslips and early purple orchids).

It is possible that the consequences of over-production of food in the EC will, over the next few years, have a major effect on the economics of land use in the Peak District. Should this happen, there would inevitably be a major change in the scenery which we now regard as characteristic of the Peak District. The most likely effect would be a reduction in pasture land and a growth of forest cover.

More Walks by Rivers and Canals:

If you enjoyed this book, look out for Tony Stephens' next book:

NORTH COUNTRY RIVER VALLEY WALKS – due Spring 1997

plus . . .

WATERWAY WALKS AROUND BIRMINGHAM – David Perrott

WATERWAY WALKS IN LEICESTERSHIRE & RUTLAND – Paul Biggs

NORTH-WEST WATERWAY WALKS: NORTH OF THE MERSEY – Dennis Needham

NORTH-WEST WATERWAY WALKS: SOUTH OF THE MERSEY – Guy Lawson

NORTH -WEST WATERWAY WALKS: THE MERSEY WATERWAYS – David Parry

. . . all at £6.95

Country Walking:

SECRET YORK: WALKS WITHIN THE CITY WALLS – Les Pierce (£6.95)

PUB WALKS IN THE YORKSHIRE DALES – Clive Price (£6.95)

PUB WALKS ON THE NORTH YORK MOORS & COAST – Stephen Rickerby (£6.95)

PUB WALKS IN THE YORKSHIRE WOLDS – Tony Whittaker (£6.95)

BEST PUB WALKS IN & AROUND SHEFFIELD – Clive Price (£6.95)

BEST PUB WALKS IN SOUTH YORKSHIRE – Martin Smith (£6.95)

THE LAKELAND SUMMITS – Tim Synge (£7.95)

100 LAKE DISTRICT HILL WALKS – Gordon Brown (£7.95)

LAKELAND ROCKY RAMBLES: Geology beneath your feet – Brian Lynas (£7.95)

FULL DAYS ON THE FELLS: Challenging Walks – Adrian Dixon (£7.95)

PUB WALKS IN THE LAKE DISTRICT – Neil Coates (£6.95)

YORKSHIRE DALES WALKING: ON THE LEVEL – Norman Buckley (£6.95)

LAKELAND WALKING, ON THE LEVEL – Norman Buckley *(£6.95)*

STROLLING WITH STEAM : walks along the Keswick Railway – Jan Darrall *(£4.95)*

TEA SHOP WALKS IN THE LAKE DISTRICT – Jean Patefield *(£6.95)*

MOSTLY DOWNHILL: LEISURELY WALKS, LAKE DISTRICT – Alan Pears *(£6.95)*

MOSTLY DOWNHILL IN THE PEAK DISTRICT – Clive Price *(£6.95)*
(two volumes, White Peak & Dark Peak)

EAST CHESHIRE WALKS – Graham Beech *(£5.95)*

WEST CHESHIRE WALKS – Jen Darling *(£5.95)*

WELSH WALKS: Dolgellau /Cambrian Coast – L. Main & M. Perrott *(£5.95)*

WELSH WALKS: Aberystwyth & District – L. Main & M. Perrott *(£5.95)*

WALKS IN MYSTERIOUS WALES – Laurence Main *(£7.95)*

RAMBLES IN NORTH WALES – Roger Redfern *(£6.95)*

PUB WALKS IN SNOWDONIA – Laurence Main *(£6.95)*

RAMBLES AROUND MANCHESTER – Mike Cresswell *(£5.95)*

FIFTY CLASSIC WALKS IN THE PENNINES – Terry Marsh *(£8.95)*

WEST PENNINE WALKS – Mike Cresswell *(£5.95)*

Cycling . . .

CYCLE UK! The essential guide to leisure cycling – Les Lumsdon *(£9.95)*

OFF-BEAT CYCLING IN THE PEAK DISTRICT – Clive Smith *(£6.95)*

MORE OFF-BEAT CYCLING IN THE PEAK DISTRICT – Clive Smith *(£6.95)*

CYCLING IN THE LAKE DISTRICT – John Wood *(£7.95)*

50 BEST CYCLE RIDES IN CHESHIRE – Graham Beech *(£7.95)*

CYCLING IN NOTTINGHAMSHIRE – Penny & Bill Howe *(£7.95)*

CYCLING IN SCOTLAND & N.E. ENGLAND – Philip Routledge *(£7.95)*

CYCLING IN NORTH WALES – Philip Routledge *(£7.95) ... available 1996*

Sport . . .

RED FEVER: from Rochdale to Rio as 'United' supporters – Steve Donoghue *(£7.95)*

UNITED WE STOOD: unofficial history of the Ferguson years – Richard Kurt *(£6.95)*

DESPATCHES FROM OLD TRAFFORD – Richard Kurt *(£6.95)*

MANCHESTER CITY: Moments to Remember – John Creighton *(£9.95)*

AN A-Z OF MANCHESTER CITY – Dean Hayes *(£6.95)*

Northern England folklore & heritage:

SHADOWS: A NORTHERN INVESTIGATION OF THE UNKNOWN – Steve Cliffe *(£7.95)*

DARK TALES OF OLD CHESHIRE – Angela Conway *(£6.95)*

CHESHIRE: ITS MAGIC & MYSTERY – Doug Pickford *(£7.95)*

GHOSTS, TRADITIONS & LEGENDS OF LANCASHIRE – Ken Howarth *(£7.95)*

JOURNEY THROUGH LANCASHIRE – Kenneth Fields *(£7.95)*

OLD NOTTINGHAMSHIRE REMEMBERED – Keith Taylor *(£7.95)*

STRANGE SOUTH YORKSHIRE – David Clarke *(£6.95)*

TRADITIONAL PUBS OF OLD LANCASHIRE – Peter Barnes *(£7.95)*

- plus many more entertaining and educational books being regularly added to our list. All of our books are available from your local bookshop. In case of difficulty, or to obtain our complete catalogue, please contact:

Sigma Leisure, 1 South Oak Lane, Wilmslow, Cheshire SK9 6AR
Phone: 01625 – 531035   Fax: 01625 – 536800

ACCESS and VISA orders welcome – call our friendly sales staff or use our 24 hour Answerphone service! Most orders are despatched on the day we receive your order – you could be enjoying our books in just a couple of days. Please add £2 p&p to all orders.